PRAISE FOR JOSEPH HARRISON'S POETRY

SOMEONE ELSE'S NAME

"Joseph Harrison's outstanding first book of poems ... reads like many good poets' third or fourth one. It is marked by a rare stylistic authority and imaginative energy, and by what one critic has praised as the mutual animation of deep poetic learning and passionate responses to immediate experience' that his poems reveal." — Citation for Academy Award in Literature from the American Academy of Arts and Letters

"Sad and funny by turns and often simultaneously, the quests, meditations, and laments in this rich collection are unfailingly sane—no, more than sane, wise. Furthermore, Harrison's every poem is lullingly melodic, though each sings a different tune. This exceptional debut is a rare delight." — Rachel Hadas

"Mr. Harrison's technique never fails him, his capacity for conveying the deepest and most subtle feelings is sure and accurate. Best of all, in every poem here, irrespective of mood or weight, the reader will encounter the sheer joy of a poet gladdened by his own art, alive to the liberties and limits of form and imagination—playful, serious, gifted, multi-vocal, and athletically adroit." — Anthony Hecht, from his Introduction to *Someone Else's Name*

"The poems in this first book are so witty and formally adept, so technically accomplished, that they almost seem to have come from another era." — Edward Hirsch

"In this brilliant first book the deepest of feeling and the most profound thought rise up in response to a glittering surface of wit, which is never an end in itself ... Mr. Harrison's imagination is unflagging, and can keep going through 'As If,' a splendid revisionary sonnet sequence, or the remarkable 'Mobile Bay Jubilee.' His is an outstanding talent, and he does not betray it by anything but the most meticulous of workmanship." — John Hollander

"Joseph Harrison ... is entertaining because he has so brilliantly mastered the formalities of English versifying. His great gift ... is for 'play,' and it's the way Harrison plays with both form and meaning that constitutes the charm of *Someone Else's Name* ... Its presiding genius is really Shakespeare, a mentor Harrison seems almost to challenge in a sequence of twenty-two linked sonnets ... In his post-modern way, Harrison all but outbids Shakespeare ... There's a good deal going on under his fancy dress." — Anne Stevenson, *London Magazine*

PRAISE FOR JOSEPH HARRISON'S POETRY

"*Someone Else's Name* is a first book full of stunning performances, each one infused with wit, feeling, and humanity, and each one delighting in the full use of the medium and its devices. It's a happy thing to witness the emergence of such a talent." — Richard Wilbur

IDENTITY THEFT

"Joseph Harrison's new volume is a wonderful leap in his poetic development. Harrison fuses formal control with a rich interiority and composes many poems that deserve to become canonical." — Harold Bloom

"[Harrison] is a consummate craftsman ... He uses language with exquisite precision to register the erosion of language, and in this ... he is both irrepressibly humorous and scathingly satirical. Harrison is a poet of great formal flamboyance. There seems to be no measure, no verse-form, at which he is not quite utterly dazzling. His poems exhibit a resonant awareness of the entire tradition of English verse and he's not diffident about displaying it. If he revels in echoes, these are mastered echoes, audaciously launched both in homage to tradition and its defence ... Perhaps it will sound solemn to call ... Joseph Harrison [a poet] by vocation. But the wit, the beauty, and the brilliant strangeness of [his] poems—perhaps even [his] inspired mischief—come with the calling. And luckily for us, [he's] ... 'having a good time.'" — Eric Ormsby, *Standpoint*

"How deeply satisfying it is to read a poet whose meditative, elegiac temperament is married happily to verbal wit, even laugh-out-loud humor. Joseph Harrison is that rare poet, one whose command of craft suits him equally to produce a two-line 'Ode' ('O elevated visionary thoughts, / Where are you now?') and a ten-page public poem ('To George Washington in Baltimore') on that American giant who understood the 'human scale.' A poet so giddy with wordplay that he dares to rhyme 'my palm is piloted' with 'Pontius Pilated' and 'pirated,' Harrison addresses nonetheless the most serious concerns. Wary of our technology-dominated present and future, in which 'identity theft' is no joke (and 'what fave new world is beckoning?'), Harrison makes his fingerprint evident in all of these poems—an implicit affirmation of something unique in each of us." — Mary Jo Salter

"The title poem of Joseph Harrison's second book is a witty and headlong discussion of how one's self, if any, is constituted. We are a patchwork, it

PRAISE FOR JOSEPH HARRISON'S POETRY

develops, and the same might be said of Harrison's book, which makes continual and expert use of Spenser, Wordsworth, Horace, Villon, and other predecessors. If this makes *Identity Theft* seem a three-ring circus, the important point is that Harrison is a superlative ringmaster: his book throughout is governed by that playfulness and performance which, as Frost said, are required in poetry however impassioned or serious. I found myself particularly moved by 'Who They Were,' which recalls the poet's mother and father in the stanza of Tennyson's 'In Memoriam.'" — Richard Wilbur

SHAKESPEARE'S HORSE

"Joseph Harrison's poetry is modern without being modernist. That is, he employs the tools and materials of traditional poetry to construct a kind of verse that is appealingly new, yet never transgressively so. His poems reflect a renewed lustre in our direction, and we come away deeply refreshed." — John Ashbery

"*Shakespeare's Horse* is Joseph Harrison's full emergence as his poet, still in the eloquent and formal tradition of Richard Wilbur and Anthony Hecht but with an accent now pitched in a new mode. Among the book's triumphs are 'Wakefield,' the wonderful 'Dr Johnson Rolls Down a Hill,' 'Damon,' and 'Harrison's Clock.' Yet I take a particular joy in the brief but enigmatic 'Hamlet' and the remarkable title sonnet. The kind of comedy that Harrison works into his subtle meditations is refreshingly original. Should he further refine his already agile art, there will be no one in his American generation who so challenges the eye and the ear to come together." — Harold Bloom

"The poems in ... *Shakespeare's Horse* might best be dubbed encyclopoetry. These are poems steeped in learning, in history, in facts .... Take 'Dr. Johnson Rolls Down a Hill,' among the volume's finest poems. One can read the poem without knowing much more than Johnson's reputation as the Great English Critic who looms over the canon with a discerning eye. Harrison's poem spells out its own occasion, with a first stanza emphasizing that 'Even a man of voluminous gravity,' 'Who relished with dispatch and enormous zest / Huge stacks of pancakes, bottomless pots of tea, / ... Contains in his heart of hearts a little boy / Who played and played all day.' And so we are led through the heavy vagaries of Johnson's life, only to find ourselves at a scene (a real one, in fact) where Johnson is with company at the top of hill. He 'divests himself of pencil, keys, and purse' and then simply lets himself roll down the hill 'As if the good life really were this easy, / As if the nightmare of

PRAISE FOR JOSEPH HARRISON'S POETRY

his coming breakdown / Had no more substance than a child's bad dream.' It's a moving passage, and one that shows the formidable Johnson's melancholy, human side. This poem, like almost every poem in the volume, is written in fluid meter. Many of them rhyme, as well. Harrison's attitude about form seems like the opposite of Robert Lowell's, who wanted rhyme and meter to look hard, and who wrote as though form were a way of showing the seriousness of your message. Harrison is more like Yeats; he makes form look easy, and his poems are better for it ..." — Joey Frantz, *The Hopkins Review*

SOMETIMES I DREAM THAT I AM NOT WALT WHITMAN

"In his brilliant, entertaining, dark, and companionable new book, Joseph Harrison, one of American poetry's best kept secrets, channels the voices and spirits of dead poets as wide ranging and diverse as Mark Strand, Emily Dickinson, Robert Frost, Wallace Stevens, and Walt Whitman himself. But Harrison never merely ventriloquizes these and other voices; or if he does the ventriloquism, as he implies in his amazing sequence, 'The Compromised Ventriloquist,' is reciprocal—such that, as he says elsewhere in the book, 'every transformation / Becomes another act of self-creation.' This book obliterates the dichotomies of self-expression and impersonality, personal disclosure and self-effacement, tradition and innovation. In the place of such facile and misleading oppositions Harrison has written a book that engages the particularities of our moment with a hawk's eye view of linguistic, metrical, and cultural history. The imagination that animates these poems is intimate and vatic, prophetic and mundane, scientific and fantastic; the music is all his own yet everyone's, 'dark and deep / And cold as interstellar night while unforgettably humane.' I love this book." — Alan Shapiro

"In Joseph Harrison's hands, verse is an art, a living art, and a generous one. 'The dead keep singing,' he writes in 'River of Song,' and they do in the lyric ventriloquism through these pages: Frost, Auden, Stevens, Dickinson, Baudelaire, Hardy, Shakespeare, and most surprisingly, Whitman. Harrison's tight forms gesture toward psychic volcanos and hurricanes, and his rhymes deploy lethal wit, as in 'Runaway Blimp,' about a military-industrial boondoggle where 'a multi-billion dollar clusterfuck' clicks with 'run amok.' His dexterities don't just serve satire; the poems play a wide scale of feelings: tenderness, wonder, wry meditation, indignation, and fury. A selfless book, in the best sense." — Rosanna Warren

"His suite of cannily resonant imitations of the good gray poet notwithstand-

PRAISE FOR JOSEPH HARRISON'S POETRY

ing, Joseph Harrison is indeed not Walt Whitman, nor does he seek to be but his verse responds eloquently to the ardent prediction in *Democratic Vistas* that the 'highest poems' to come would spring from 'the assumption that the process of reading is ... in the highest sense, an exercise, a gymnast's struggle.' Harrison's intensely wrought poems reward the reader well beyond the demands they make. Ebullient yet concentrated products of an audacious prosodist and syntactician, an exhilarating logophile and a master of tone, they evince a maker's maker. A set of poems in Emily Dickinson's mode balances the Whitman suite, and Frost and Stevens, Yeats and Auden and Merrill ghost happily through this volume, itself a 'unity of network.' It compasses 'structures of posed placidity' — structures that arise, we come to know, from an 'intemperate liquidity / Whose outbursts, unpredictable, reveal / A flare for the dramatic.'" — Stephen Yenser

COLLECTED POEMS

ALSO BY JOSEPH HARRISON

POETRY

Someone Else's Name
(Zoo, Waywiser, 2003)

Identity Theft
(Waywiser, 2008)

The Fly in the Ointment
(Syllabic, 2014)

Shakespeare's Horse (
Waywiser, 2015)

The Imposition of Ashes: Early Poems
(Syllabic, 2016)

Sometimes I Dream That I Am Not Walt Whitman
(Waywiser, 2020)

EDITOR

Un mondo che non può essere migliore: Poesie scelte 1956-2007
— with Damiano Abeni —
(Luca Sossella Editore, 2008)

The Hecht Prize Anthology: 2005–2009
(Waywiser, 2011)

JOSEPH HARRISON

COLLECTED POEMS

WAYWISER

First published in 2024 by

THE WAYWISER PRESS

Christmas Cottage, Church Enstone, Chipping Norton, Oxfordshire, OX7 4NN, UK
6419 Cedonia Avenue, Baltimore, MD 21206, USA
https://waywiser-press.com

Editor-in-Chief
Philip Hoy

Senior American Editor
Joseph Harrison

Associate Editors
Katherine Hollander | Eric McHenry | Dora Malech | V. Penelope Pelizzon
Clive Watkins | Greg Williamson | Matthew Yorke

Copyright © Joseph Harrison, 2024

The right of Joseph Harrison to be identified as the author of this work
has been asserted by him in accordance with the
Copyright, Designs and Patents Act of 1988.

All rights reserved. No part of this publication may be reproduced, stored in a retrieval
system, or transmitted in any form or by any means, electronic, mechanical, photocopying,
recording, or otherwise, without the prior permission of both the copyright owner and the
above publisher of this book.

The poems in this collection originally appeared in the following works:

Someone Else's Name (Zoo Press, Waywiser, 2003)
Identity Theft (Waywiser, 2008)
Shakespeare's Horse, (Waywiser, 2015)
Sometimes I Dream That I Am Not Walt Whitman (Waywiser, 2020)

9 7 5 3 1 2 4 6 8

A CIP catalogue record for this book is available from the British Library

Hardback ISBN 978-1-911379-14-0
Paperback ISBN 978-1-911379-15-7

Printed and bound by
T. J. Books Ltd., Padstow, Cornwall, PL28 8RW

CONTENTS

SOMEONE ELSE'S NAME

I. Songs and Sonnets

All That's Left	23
The Beautiful Peephole	25
The Cretonnes of Penelope	26
Variation on a Theme by the Weather	27
Song	29
Sunshine and Rain	31
On a Line by Wyatt	32
The Lover His Complaint	33
From the Songbook of Henri Provence	34
As If	36

II. Stories

Holly Nova Regrets	49
Dante in Erebus	50
Donal Russell Unbound	53
Like Two Men in a Boat	56
The Eccentric Traveler	59
Air Larry	62
Dante Lost	64
The End of Dewitt Finley	66

III. Signs and Figures

Frost Heaves	75
Not Playing Possum	77
Lost Punctles	78
A Different Bird	79
Catoptric	81
The Relic	82
At the Grave of Burns	84
In the Protestant Cemetery in Rome	86
Looking for the Lama	87
View of Baltimore from Green Mount Cemetery	89
Peregrine Falcon on Skyscraper	96
Checkered Present	100
Words on Words	102
Young Will Shakespeare	103
Mobile Bay Jubilee	106

CONTENTS

IDENTITY THEFT

I. Trajectories

The Catch	117
Identity Theft	120
Virtual Death	125
Hikikomori	127
Trajectory	129
The Last Book	130

II. Odes and Elegies

Elegy	133
Ode	134
For a Season	135
For the Old Women	136
To False Spring	137
On a Porcelain Bowl	138
To a House Sparrow	139
On Lethargy	140
For an Apple Tree	141
To the Wind	142
Intimations	143
For Donald Justice	145
For Anthony Hecht	146
On Rereading Some Lines of Poetry	147
Who They Were	150

III. Tropes

Ship of Trope	163
Gum	164
Touch and Go	165
Paper View	168
A Spade a Spade	174
Nautical Terms	177
To an Aldabran Tortoise, Dead at 250	183
To Amaryllis	186
To the Republic	187
To George Washington in Baltimore	188
To My Friends	196

CONTENTS

SHAKESPEARE'S HORSE

To C	201

⁜

Windsock	205
To Pluto, Upon Its Declassification	207
Afghan Kites	210

⁜

Wakefield	214

⁜

To Quintus Minimus	221
To Gallienus	222
To Aeneas Silvius on Monte Amiata	223

⁜

Dr. Johnson Rolls Down a Hill	226

⁜

Henri Provence in Wessex	230
Larkin's Nephew	232
Oh	233

⁜

Sunday Evening	235

⁜

The Site	238
The Key	240
The Place	241

⁜

Sparse Rhymes	245

⁜

Archibald Leach	250
He Wasn't Proust	251
Portrait of the Artist as a Young Kid	253

CONTENTS

✝

Damon	256

✝

To Riccardo Duranti	262
To Barack Obama	264
To His Book	266

✝

To Trebitsch Lincoln in Hell	268

✝

Sky Burial	281
Hearing Voices	282
King Lear	283

✝

Hamlet	285

✝

Ice Age Art	287
Fidelities	288
Harrison's Clock	291

✝

Shakespeare's Horse	299

CONTENTS

SOMETIMES I DREAM THAT I AM NOT WALT WHITMAN

River of Song   305

I.

Derecho   309
Stopping   310
Echolocation   311
Orogenesis   312
Autopoiesis   314
The Demon Dinanukht   315
Mark Strand   316
The End Was Over   317

II.

Elegy for the American Sublime   318
Sometimes I Dream That I Am Not Walt Whitman   321
Let Them Say Whatever They Want   322
Returning to the Sea-shore   323
I Hear It Is Charged Against Me   324
Like a Ghost I Returned   325
Some Tuesdays I Go to Lisbon   326
My Old Camerado, My Body   327

III.

Runaway Blimp   331
Song of the NRA   334
Easter 2016   335
The Retreat   336
Coulrophobia with Line from Auden   338

IV.

Plein Air   341
The Ekphrastic Poet   342
Harvest Hobson   343
The Albatross   345
Giotto in Padua   346
Velázquez in Rome   347
Cézanne in Baltimore   348
The Compromised Ventriloquist   349

CONTENTS

V.

"My Sister Cut Me into Pieces"	355
"A Room of Zombies Smiled at Me"	356
"It's What's Inside Estranges Most"	357
"You'll Pay to Quote a Word of Mine"	358
"I Would Have Loathed Publicity"	359

VI.

"You Haven't Heard the End of Me"	360
Hardy's Writing Trousers	363
The Forsaken Singer	364
Aubade	365
Late Autumnal	366
Hobson's Choice	367
On Time	368
Shakespeare's Head	369

VII.

Dickens on Fire	377

* * *

INDEX OF TITLES	387
INDEX OF FIRST LINES	391
ACKNOWLEDGMENTS	395
A NOTE ABOUT THE AUTHOR	397

SOMEONE ELSE'S NAME

though the Essence of Poetry may indeed be chiefly Lyricall, given the compression and fluctuation of the Passions afforded by sonets and other pretty forms ... still the Narratives of men's Misfortunes influence us in a graver Manner, especially as their trials seem to bear some Kinship to our own Troubles ... but finally all Poetry Lyricall, Pastorall, Dramatick & Narrative, yields its intended Purpose and succumbs to the intoxicating Proliferation of Figure ... who are we even to prick the paper's playne (as sayd the poet, *A Gentil Knight* etc.) when the Signes themselves point which way they please, and our most carefull Significcacioun is twisted in the confusions of Allegorickall Interpretation?

The Arte of English Poesie, Bk. IV, ch. ix

I. Songs and Sonnets

ALL THAT'S LEFT

Will someone tell me, please,

Who carved these trees
With someone else's name?

These woods won't be the same,
For I thought, all along,

Mine was the only signature among
These pale textures of bark

Rising out of the dark
Underworld of the forest floor.

But who was here before?
Who chiseled each new line

On everything I thought was mine,
Initialling all these

Purely imaginary trees
Deep in the forest of my mind?

No Orlando, mad for Rosalind:
These cuttings, even when crude,

Speak only out of solitude,
The signs of a single heart

That gave its love to art
And wore *that* on its sleeve,

Having come to believe
It was the necessary sacrifice,

And paid the price.
If someone else could see

ALL THAT'S LEFT

These careful lines, would he,
Underneath their curlicue and flair,

Hear the real pathos there,
The note of the ultimate cost

When feeling itself is lost
And all that's left is the mark

Of absence against the dark?

THE BEAUTIFUL PEEPHOLE

The beautiful peephole lets us see the way
The others live, and they live lavishly,
Blowing their soft-won millions on a spree.
If we could be them, only for a day!

The beautiful peephole shows us the high style,
Champagne and velvet, the stretch limousine,
The latest sprinklings in the new cuisine—
Not ours, not even for a little while.

The beautiful peephole lets us see into
The dressing rooms of stars, and lets us see
The star herself undressing carelessly
Until a mechanism shuts the view,

But not before we've taken in the scope
Of all we'll never have, the thrills, the laughs,
Savannahs full of emus and giraffes,
And swallowed a little poison pill of hope

Whose toxins start to glaze the inner eye
Through which we see our ordinary lives,
The same old jobs and problems, husbands and wives,
With shimmers of the possibility

It could be altogether otherwise.
And that slight sparkle changes how we feel
About ourselves and all we know is real.
We close our hearts up, and we feast our eyes.

THE CRETONNES OF PENELOPE

How stupid Penelope's suitors must have been,
Each morning as they elbowed for a place
Near her, and cocked their wits, eyeing each other,
Never to notice yesterday's tapestry
Had disappeared, like every day's before.

They kept maneuvering, and they kept score,
Each scheming to get the better of his brother.
So each day's small creation went unseen
Unless some maid in waiting saw that face
Glancing from corners of the tapestry.

She wove a glimpse of him in every scene
She patterned on the vanishing tapestry.
Nor did it have to be obliquely traced
To fool the fools not looking anymore,
Who couldn't tell one figure from another.

But if this game was all, she wanted more,
One friend (it wouldn't have to be a lover)
Who saw how the resourceful tapestry's
Long lesson in how never quite to mean
Inscribed the careful lines upon her face.

At night when she ripped up the tapestry
She felt she'd run a marathon in place.
Her sole delight was her most painful chore.
She knew she couldn't make it new again.
But when the sun came up she started over.

VARIATION ON A THEME BY THE WEATHER

On the radio today they estimated
The chance of rain at one hundred percent,
    Which seems exaggerated
Given a world where chance outruns prediction
And every day some unforetold event
    Proves certainty a fiction,

Where walls that severed continents collapse
Not from the exercise of stockpiled might,
    But through the gradual lapse
Of purpose in the fabricated state
That can't get elemental functions right,
    And history can't wait,

Where favorites blow overwhelming leads,
And politicians who are on the take
    Do civic-minded deeds,
Where patients terminally ill survive,
And under the rubble of a huge earthquake
    One child is found alive,

And the most watched of variable things
Is weather which is mostly unforeseeable,
    A flow of moods and swings
That parades its perfect days, then flaunts its flaws,
Lurching from mild to disagreeable
    In sync with unruly laws

To form incalculable permutations,
Fractal patterns rippling outward through
    So many iterations
That our precise computers merely show,
For all we know now that we never knew,
    Chance limits what we know.

VARIATION ON A THEME BY THE WEATHER

Yet given a swerving universe where pure
Uncertainty extends so vast a rule
    That nothing else seems sure,
In this particular case I do know how
One might say, without sounding like a fool,
    It's going to rain: it's raining now.

SONG

Like the first cold trickles to slip
    Between blue shingles of shale
High on a famous mountainside,
    To run and pool and spill
    And, "echoing down the vale,"
      Spread far and wide,

Like the first gray gull to appear
    As the light fades, and sail
Past the tall buildings, floating home
    To the harbor's storied repair,
    Till, dot by dot, without fail,
      The birds come,

Like the first tipped prong to unfold
    A tentative hint of white
Against the green of the fabled tree
    (Where once such fruit fell down!),
    Which will, in days, ignite
      Quite suddenly

Pale tier upon tier of apple blossom,
    Loading its limbs and curling
Fingers, like and unlike the snow
    That packed the tree with snow-bloom
    During the freak storm swirling
      Just days ago,

So the idea for the poem
    Starts with a layered phrase,
A story, a simile, a sleight,
    And though the poet may mope
    Through the flat, vacant days,
      Or cry at night

SONG

    For the lightning he almost believes
        Struck him once, long ago
(When mind was fire, and heart was song),
        Something won't leave him be,
        But mumbles, liquid, slow,
            And pulls him along

To where the desk juts like a cliff
        Above the original sea,
And the white wings flash in the sun,
        And a light comes on with a flick,
        And clear, emphatic, free,
            The words come.

SUNSHINE AND RAIN

Just walking along the street this warm spring day,
    Liking the sunshine, when—what's this,
A raindrop? And another, certainly rain,
The fundamental contraries at play,

> *You have seen sunshine*
> *And rain at once*

The colloquy of genius with a dunce,
    Or pleasure's argument with pain,
A fight that ends abruptly in a kiss
As Chastity turns Mistress of the Hunts,

> *Her smiles and tears*
> *Were like a better way*

The glass of water with the glass of wine,
    The vocal days, the silent years,
Wisdom and folly mingling like King Lear's
As words from long ago fill up this line.

ON A LINE BY WYATT

It was no dream, I lay broad waking
And love was mine, there for the taking,
    Naked and warm,
Without the fear of what we might be making
    Or a thought to its form.

It was no dream, I lay broad waking.
So what was real? And who was faking?
And what did you mean by that "how like you this"?
I saw you from a distance, I'm still shaking.
I swear I'll never write to you again,
You who were both Scylla and Charybdis
    Of whom I still complain.

THE LOVER HIS COMPLAINT

You left me years ago, and ever since,
In every single person I have seen,
I've just seen they weren't you. It makes no sense.

Why should the thought of you still make me wince,
The thought of you with someone turn me green?
You left me years ago—forever, since

There's no way back to where we were. Past tense,
Past thought, as if the whole thing hadn't been
And wasn't me or you. It makes no sense

To go on dreaming on you. I'm no prince,
If sometimes, in my mind's eye, you're a queen
Darkened by tragedy, and ever since

Compelled to pay back some austere absence
With sacrifices that are never clean,
Witness this missive. But it makes no sense,

A letter posted nowhere, like footprints
In snow that simply stop. In some such scene
You left me years ago, and ever since
I've stood there waiting, and it makes no sense.

FROM THE SONGBOOK OF HENRI PROVENCE

1

Arrival of the insects, and the green
    Protrusions of renewal,
As light turns on a switch, and the whole scene
    Springs back to life, and all
That world of ice and snow, austere, pristine,
    And hard as any jewel,
Seems nothing now, melted to having been
    And farther off than fall.

2

The thick and sweaty air, the pounding sun,
    The miasmal steam that rises
From asphalt, track, and pasture, overcome
    The simplest exercises,
Leaving us flopped on couches, listless, numb,
    And stunned that spring's surprises,
The miracles we numbered one by one,
    Led to such strict assizes.

3

The whirligig of leaves, the sick-sweet scent
    Of fallen apples rotting,
The swift encroachment of the sun's descent
    On afternoons, the plotting
Of store and pantry shelves, crammed with intent,
    The Vs of geese, the nutting,
Make us forget those months that seemed hell-sent
    As if their trials were nothing.

FROM THE SONGBOOK OF HENRI PROVENCE

4

And now the world's a blank page, frozen hard
    As disbelief, extreme
As absence, blanketing the small back yard
    In flash and fitful gleam,
Concealing the cold earth we worked and scarred
    Till harvest comes to seem
A distant pageant in which we humans starred
    Only in some dim dream.

AS IF

1

Let me begin, as if there never were
Whole sequences of pyrotechnic verse
Flashing the features of some him or her,
Implying all the meanwhile, what is worse,
That all is just projection, that the fame
Offered the bright beloved, age by age,
Laura or Stella or some other name,
Sparkles and dazzles only on the page.
O let me start, as if the mind were free
Of all those pretty rooms and polished turns
That flip their figures so predictably
We know what freezes will become what burns,
As if these lines could stammer something true
To someone real, as if there were a you.

2

And if there were, I knew you long before
I saw your face or heard your name, your eyes
Were from some childhood dream, where angels rise
To blend in air, and there they were, and poor,
Awkward me, stuttering in the schoolhouse door,
All subject lost, all utterances lies,
A heart puffed up to twenty times its size
And blown to pieces—what was I asking for?
To be, in all known senses, so possessed
By waves of love (or was it lust?) that all
That's left of self is thoroughly dispossessed
Of all its sense? That wasn't it, at all.
And I thought you were someone I could choose,
Not just be chosen by. "Fool," said my muse.

AS IF

3

Look in my heart, what's left of it, and write
The honest declarations that just might
Move you to love me, even for one night,
If I could only get the phrasing right?
If I could only get the phrasing right
I'd take your hand in candelabra light
And step by step ascend the spiral flight
Of marble stairs—or are they chrysolite?
Oh, I can never get the phrasing right!
There is no text, much less a copyright,
And all's been said much better than I might.
I'll sleep alone, like every other night.
Belaurelled lovers hold their dream girls tight
And all I do is write.

4

And all I do is wrong, or so it seems,
Discovering a little bit too late
That you have grown impatient with my schemes.
I should have kissed you on the second date
And all would have been perfect. In my dreams.
I'd love you, lady, at a lower rate
If that would help. I'd take it to extremes,
Send flowers daily, then send chocolate,
And book us flights to Paris, where we'd go
Sauntering down the boulevards, and sip
Expensive wines. I'd take it fast, or slow,
And foot the bill for everything, and tip
With suave largesse. Tuxedoed for the show,
I lead you to our opera box. And trip.

AS IF

5

And fall and winter come and go, and spring
Begins to hatch a world now on the wing,
Inquisitive of every opening flower.
Now as if programmed by some scripting power
The couples couple, in their own good time.
They pair off just like metaphors for rhyme,
Vanilla chocolate swirls of yin and yang.
It all comes back, just like a boomerang.
And I sit, cataleptic, in the park,
On the one bench in shadow, until dark,
And seem, no doubt, to lovers strolling past
A solitary loser, rightly cast
As odd man out, or merely looked right through,
A no one never being seen with you.

6

One scene with you is all I'd ask to play:
I'd ham it up, I'd play it to the hilt
And make it run forever and a day.
I'd praise your virtue, and thus tweak your guilt.
I'd trot out all the clever toys I've built
For you alone, I'd sing, I'd stop the show
And all the profs from Yale to Vanderbilt
Would write us up as classics: all would know
Us as the real McCoy; each cameo
You make in the long sequence would be hailed
A stellar turn ("too bad the guy's named Joe");
They'd marvel my contraptions never failed.
One last plea brings the house down. I discover
You in the wings with Astrophel, your lover.

AS IF

7

Your lover is a problem, I'll admit.
I know I cannot match his gift, his scope
(He frequents prostitutes, he peddles dope),
Much less his publications (he's a shit):
He's all hooked in where I am all locked out
(I wonder you don't notice he's a bore;
At writing school they called him "Running Sore"—
Perhaps he cleared that up). I have no doubt
That his high ship of great verse, bound for you
(As self-regard puffs out its paper sails)
And contemporary readers, never fails
To meet today's aesthetic (flat and "true"—
Too true to be good). I see why he's your man
(His poems aren't metaphors, and they don't scan).

8

Don't scan the pages of the magazines
For news of you and me: all that I write
Slips through the cracks, and nothing sees the light.
My credits don't amount to a hill of beans.
My canon is a stack of might-have-beens,
Assembled, with long labor, bit by bit.
A tree fell, but nobody noticed it.
Attack a windmill and the windmill wins.
But in this loss there's something to be gained
Precisely because nothing is in store:
Since these lines clearly won't serve other ends
You'll know my dumb devotion is not feigned.
The game is fixed. I know I'll never score
But send these, quietly, to my private friends.

AS IF

9

My private friends all tell me I'm a fool
To moon and pine, and mope about the house
In underwear; they're tired of hearing me grouse
About you and the others; it's uncool,
They say, to set my sights so high (or low,
As some would have it) then to bum and pout
When, not surprisingly, things don't work out.
They all agree on this. What do they know?
They don't know you, not well enough to say
That were they in my pickle they'd just move
On to some other interest. Anyway,
Who's asking them? I've got something to prove,
If only to myself. The only way
I know to love you is to stay in love.

10

And stay in love I have, now for so long
It's hard for me to remember the distant time
When you weren't all I wanted. Am I wrong
To keep obsessing like this? Is it a crime
To prop my house of cards up rhyme by rhyme,
Holding my breath, suspecting all along
That someone quintessentially sublime
Circles in circles where I don't belong?
I wish it were. I would confess my guilt
And plead for the heavy sentence I'd deserve,
Applaud conviction, dutifully serve,
Just so you'd see the edifice I've built
Of absence, air, and you, just so you'd see
You've had a lover from the start. Yes, me.

AS IF

11

Me me me me: must all flow through the prism
Of vitreous, primary narcissism?
Is selfhood all we're wrapped up in, so wound
In layers of reaction, of defense
(The child within nursing his troubled sense
Of who he was and is, each early wound
Malforming and definitive and who
He always will be, sulking, deep inside),
That everything is ego, through and through?
There must be more. There must be. I have tried
Imagining someone else along for the ride,
Imagining someone I am writing to.
(I've called and called. I've written notes. I've cried.)
An editor? An audience? No, you.

12

Know you are always in my mind and heart
Where we are both together and apart.
When sunrise sweeps the sky from gray to blue
Or, shedding clouds, the moon steps into view
I feel you, yes, I almost see you there.
Something is rising, current, in the air.
Or sometimes, in the midst of urban noise,
Car horns, car engines, sirens, radios,
A silence opens up its counterpoise
And fills with what, like music, comes and goes,
Like inklings of annotation curled in rows,
And I see from the start you *were* my choice
O hall of mirrors, cavern of clear echoes,
And know I know you, even as air, pure voice.

AS IF

13

Poor voice without a body, how can you
Exist as other than a slight phantasm,
The frail projection I keep talking to,
Estranged from touch, from kiss, from joy's spasm?
I've always liked thin women, it is true,
But you're thin air, an echo across the chasm
That severs poem and subject, present and past,
The world and paradise. And there we fall.
Sometimes I think you don't exist at all,
That not a single line of this will last.
But then your footsteps come, troubling my sleep,
And I can't wake, and in the living dream
I feel you well up-pouring in a stream
Fresh and original, clear and cold and deep.

14

And cold and deep the oceanic stream
Washes me up in tatters on the shore.
I write your name: the next wave rubs it out.
Was our love some cruel deity's cruel scheme?
I know that I won't see you anymore;
I blame myself, I flounder in self-doubt,
And then your voice stops me: why can't I see
These are the scripted trials love must pass through?
Absence is presence, presence absence, you
Have from the very beginning favored me,
Whispered your secret syllables in my ear,
Coaxed me to pay your steep, rising tuition
On the chance, some distant day, of such fruition.
Then why do I still doubt you? What do I fear?

AS IF

15

I fear success. Or failure. Which is worse?
And which is which? Better not ask the purse,
It couldn't tell the difference. A first-rate book
May get remaindered—does that mean it fails
The chain bookstores, where Jewel tops the sales?
("So what's the angle, baby, where's the hook?")
Of course it might not get published at all,
Just wander in limbo, turned down everywhere.
Does it exist, then? Like you I'm thin air,
Pipe dream, cloud castle, in perpetual
Dissolve and rearrangement—all for the birds.
Then failure be my triumph! Year by year
I've artfully pursued the non-career
From the beginning, down to these very words.

16

These very words, like bells, will take their toll.
Let's at the least, Petrarchan rigmarole
Aside, admit that that's the case. The worst
Scenario, my love, for me and you,
Is that this bubble's fancy flight will burst
Before the climax we are coming to
Distrust—fireworks, the spangled sky shot through
With flare and falling sparkle—yet both desire
To hasten and postpone. The longer view,
In which we watch our ashes snuff our fire,
Would be the wiser one, no doubt. I tire
Of such exertion, come up short of breath,
No longer young, and straining to expire
At times when every line's a little death.

AS IF

17

A little death goes a long way, it's true.
Bare boughs, bare choirs, a dangling leaf or two,
My face as winter's, old as cold, each blast
Of air freezing the present in the past.
"Remember me," I mumble in the dark,
My fire consumed now to a final spark
Buried in ash. Ah, yes. That mortal pang
Gave the dark twist to all the songs we sang.
But even a single spark may have the power
To set the world on fire, at the right hour:
Conception's window opens when it's time
And deep within you two cells start to chime
And suddenly we've made a living thing.
I freak. I quail. I crow. I buy a ring.

18

And by a ring we mean to signify
Commitment, union, circularity
In love as life, the field where you and I
Turn into us, in confidence that we
Will always love us and will never lie
As one turns into two turns into three,
A circle turns a sphere, its tune our song,
Whose words are truth itself, and won't be varied.
Then one day I come home and something's wrong,
You're reeling under weight that won't be carried.
No death is little. What did not live long,
And never had a name, and won't be buried ...
We wanted what we wanted, all along.
And now it won't be, and we won't be _____.

AS IF

19

Fill in the blank with this: that you have left
Me in confusion—what did I do wrong?
It wasn't like we weren't getting along,
At least I thought we were. And now, bereft,
Bewildered, scanning each suspect word and deed
(Was this it? Was it that? The old ping-pong)
I drink and pace the stripped rooms all night long,
Dissecting a sequence I can never read.
O why can't I say something incredibly deft
To win you back? I'd sing my master song,
The very trees would weep, the stones would bleed.
But somewhere I turned right, and you turned left,
And all I thought was right was really wrong,
And now I cannot write, or even read.

20

You may not even read this; if you do,
You might not recognize yourself as "you."
It all seems long ago now, I suppose
(Although it seems like yesterday to me:
I can't believe that I'm the one you chose
Never to choose). It wasn't meant to be?
That's clear enough. I should be reconciled
To life without you, given the sleep I've lost
Tangled in sheets that twisted as I tossed
And turned more figures destined to be filed
Away as futile correspondence, styled
"Archaic, formal." How long, at what cost
Pursue a course sidereally crossed?
So why does your very mention drive me wild?

AS IF

21

"I've me wild side, still," the old moneybanks
Chuckles, but I'm stunned stupid, seeing there,
Posed on his arm, mouthing a "honey, thanks"
(Rescued from circuits of the old despair?),
Someone too much like you, with different hair.
Just now our host, a man called Bunny, cranks
The music. Not a word. A single stare.
It's you. I know. Remember the funny pranks,
The time we leafleted the dorms with news
School was suspended? But he's spotted the booze
And you sail off across the crowded room
Leaving me decked by the proverbial boom.
O vision! O delusion! And you're which?
And all I know for certain is he's rich.

22

And I am poor without you, poorer still
Without the hope of you. Do what you will,
Forget me every time you cross my street,
Deny the pact we made to love and art
And life itself as both, repress the heat
Of nights we turned to one beast, with one heart,
I won't forget. I should have let you stay
Heavenly, distant, abstract, but I thought
To ballast love: your body was my way.
I should have stuck to air, as I was taught.
And now you've got me never getting you
Through all the old scenarios so far.
You're still the void I'm always writing to.
You don't write back. But you know who you are.

II. Stories

HOLLY NOVA REGRETS

A grieving star splashes across the tabloids.
What suffering in velvet, what platinum blonde
Flashes of anger at the paparazzi!
Her blinding entourage pops off like fireworks
As she ducks darkly into the dark car.
And through the dark glass we imagine tears.

Her story is that we are told her story.
So magnified by snapshot reproduction,
Relayed by satellite, the image of
Celebrity herself, what can she feel
Intrusion doesn't offer to her fan base,
Who base the dreams they fan by watching her
On watching her implode among the stars?

In every story we read our own stories,
As if the times gave us, in daily pages,
Untimely legends we're the fractals of.
Another lost adventure; casualties.
And through the dark glass we imagine tears.

DANTE IN EREBUS

"ROBOT TO ENTER ACTIVE VOLCANO IN ANTARTICA: A walking robot named Dante is to make an unprecedented descent next month into an active Antarctic volcano." — A.P., December 1992

O TRAVELER TURN BACK WHEN YOU ARRIVE
AT THIS ICED GATE YAWNING ON MOLTEN FIRE
FOR NO MAN SHALL LEAVE EREBUS ALIVE

Will Dante, with no laurel and no lyre,
Pass such a warning on his slow descent
Into a place sufficient to inspire

Anyone but a robot to invent
Infernal images, a pit where hot
Magma shoves open its volcanic vent?

It's hard to imagine a more desolate spot—
An island at the edge of Ross Ice Shelf,
Off coasts named after Hillary and Scott—

Or trials more fitting for the bard himself
Given the differences of now from then,
The enemies not Ghibelline or Guelf

Nor layered by depravity of sin
But the wild, swirling elements at vast
Extremities inimical to men.

He'll use his eight legs to maneuver past
Corrosive acids and precipitous cliffs,
Huge lava bombs and plumes of sizzling gas,

Inching around the metamorphic rifts
And hissing fissures (such dexterity's
Not least among his technologic gifts,

Along with immortality: his lease
On life's not frail who's not alive; what's more,
He doesn't have to come back in one piece).

DANTE IN EREBUS

It's information he'll be looking for
As he creeps near the lake of lava that
Boils and bubbles on the crater floor:

Is Erebus a primal rheostat?
And does the big rip in our atmosphere
Originate in its abysmal vat?

(He's funded, partly, by the hope or fear
That nature and not man issues the threat
Now widening above us year by year.)

Plus he's in training for another feat
Which should command more press than brief side-bars:
He may brave cold as utter as this heat,

Sent in the black direction of the stars
To take the measure of obscure terrain,
The orange deserts of the planet Mars.

No matter where he's put to work again,
He'll function under certain limitations
As constant as his freedom from all pain:

Ever oblivious to implications,
Indifferent to meaning as to cold,
Incapable of dreams or machinations,

He will march on exactly as he's told;
His every careful step is automated;
He's operated by remote control.

But though his journey's programmed, it's not fated.
(Indeed, Dante was thwarted years ago:
Just like its form, this poem is outdated,

DANTE IN EREBUS

Slower than even he, and he was slow.)
No version of his quest can be official—
The visions he can't see we never know.

All our intelligence is artificial,
Filtered through his, no better than a source
Whose foremost focus must be superficial,

Negotiating such a tricky course.
This much is safe to say: even if he
Returned some day with greater skill or force,

Testing the limits of technology,
He'd have less feeling still than any fool,
And would not see, even if he could see,

Like the blind man who'd been to Dante's school
And saw the legions fallen thousandfold,
The monster rear up off the fiery pool

As from his hands in billows the flames rolled.

DONAL RUSSELL UNBOUND

In America, it all winds up in court:
Witness the case of one man, Donal Russell,
Who wished to leave something of himself behind.
He loved fly-fishing, and wrote poetry,
Shy, serious pursuits, where patience leads
To lucky spots of brief felicity.
The trick's to make the lure look natural,
A living thing, in season, twitching the water,
A waterbug, a larva, or a fly,
Then as an image rises to take the bait
Jerk the taut line—though even if something catches
Often you'll toss it back into the stream,
Too small to keep, or, if it's more substantial,
Savor the taste in private, all your own.

You eat the fish that day, and poems, well,
Their issue is even more ephemeral.
They don't get garnished with lemon and sprigs of thyme,
Consumed in a moment's relish, fresh and good,
But wander in limbo, possibilities
That disappear before they ever arrive,
Or stand a little to the side of time
And wait for someone, anyone, to come
And find them posed, immobile, on the table,
Inedible as imitation fruit.
Even if one could eat them they would taste
Different to other palates than pronounced
Their syllables in silence, long ago.

Who then can fault this man's last act of will,
To keep his words, however poor they be,
However plain their music, or derived,
In a safe place by holding them in him
Even when thought had slipped outside his mind?
So Donal Russell, of Springfield, Oregon,
Professional fly-tier, proprietor
Of Russell's Bug House (the tying of the bait
Is another art: some fishermen prefer

DONAL RUSSELL UNBOUND

To twist it with a personal signature,
Binding the fly with a lock of their own hair),
A son and lover of "the great outdoors"
Who wrote his thoughts down in what words he could,
So Donal Russell of Springfield, Oregon,
Willed that upon his death his body be
Skinned from the head down, that the skin be tanned,
Then used to face-bind volumes of his poems.

When the day came the funeral home refused,
Citing the laws of Oregon, which define
Any and all post-mortem practices
That are "not recognized by generally
Accepted standards of the community"
As criminally abusive of the corpse.
And so his family has gone to court
To plead before Judge Pierre Van Rysselberghe
That the late man's last wish be realized,
While he awaits the rule of law, embalmed,
At rest in fluid as before his birth,
His pickling flesh still covering his bones
And not his words, which wait as well, unbound,
Like those of many others, like a book
That lengthens as it waits another year
And on and on, having no place to go,
As we all wait for someone to decide
Something, so we can get on with our lives,
Or afterlives, for those who have just those.

I haven't read his poems, and I don't know
When or where or if he will be bound,
But offer this (though no one's listening,
Least of all Judge Pierre Van Rysselberghe)
As sympathetic evidence that his
Request would be quite recognizable
To communities of poets, present and past,
Who'd give their hides to see their work survive.

DONAL RUSSELL UNBOUND

Blake or Dickinson would have understood
The urge to make a book that was a thing
Unlike all other books, all other things,
Different against the living hand's soft skin.
As for the mutilation of the corpse,
That's what art does to life, stripping away
The surfaces of things to wrap itself
In all it isn't and can never be.
Donal Russell was one of the lucky ones.
Some poets, I'm afraid, get skinned alive,
Like fool Marsyas, who dared to match his skill
With true, immortal music, and was flayed
For pride, without regard for that clear style
Admired on all the local mountainsides,
Or suffer other catastrophic fates,
Like Orpheus, who got ripped limb from limb
By one last angry, partisan audience,
Though rocks and trees were moved by his dying song.
At most one hopes to work on, like Arachne,
Who lied about the sources of her gift
And saw her work defaced by the jealous Minerva
And felt herself transformed, as her head and body
Shrunk into almost nothing, but still spins
A world of intricate geometries,
Of gossamer octagons and lattices
Glistening on thin air, to catch a fly.

LIKE TWO MEN IN A BOAT

So why on earth set sail

When even the fittest craft seems bound to fail
On fickle seas,

Or drift for weeks or months without a breeze,
While overhead the big-winged birds

Circle a sky as blank as a page without words,
And every sailor wonders why he came

To sign his name
To the Quixotic roll

Of those attracted to some distant pole
As the horizon rose beyond,

Bound to the word, taking each word as bond,
Examining the charts and marking the stars

(And Venus, and Mars)
To plot a largely arbitrary course

In search of the half-mythical lost source,
Or aimed at an imaginary line

(We've saved one bottle of wine),
Then when the season changes and the big winds come

To be pushed and punished and overcome
As all hands lose their grips

And the whole thing flips,
Dumping the charts and instruments down the drink,

And as they sink
Everyone swims like hell,

LIKE TWO MEN IN A BOAT

Though no one, thrashing the ocean, can tell,
As the pain numbs first an arm, and then a leg,

If he's the gamete locked in on the egg,
Till someone staggers upright out of the foam

Onto a strange shore—home,
Like two men in a boat,

Fishing, who drifted out and proceeded to float
For weeks on the Hawaiian waterways

(The Coast Guard gave up looking after five days),
Riding the swells in their improbable craft,

Not much more than a raft,
All the way to the end of the island chain,

Eating what fish they caught and drinking rain
(That month it rained,

And rained)
Day after day,

And, amazingly, were pretty much OK
(Though they really could have used a whatchamathingy)

Till a whale upended their dinghy
And deep-sixed their gear,

And the skies turned clear,
And soon, with no way to catch food, and nothing to drink,

And their craft, beginning to sink,
In need of constant inflating,

LIKE TWO MEN IN A BOAT

With the sea bottom waiting
And no sign of shore,

Each carved farewell to his family on his oar
And prepared to be

Finally and definitively lost at sea,
Dissolving in a grave of salt and brine

Out near the International Date Line,
When a fisherman

Working off the final island
Picked them up and brought them in,

Where tales begin.

THE ECCENTRIC TRAVELER

Nature alone is perfect. In the woods
The angles of the light, crisscrossing the pines,
Portion the forest air into luminous panes
Fractured by towering shafts, and the upper boughs
Display the various tints and shades of green
Scrawled by the vines and bushes and small trees
Swarming the forest floor. All's a green blur,
And rippling through the green is a wave of song
Cresting above you, whistles and chirps and trills
Which cross and quarrel, counter and amplify,
A flowing over, spontaneous, carefree,
Implying all the purity of joy.
Then silence. Shadows alternate with sun.

Soon, in the failing light, the path begins
To grow increasingly dim, ambiguous turns
Lead nowhere fast, a path does re-emerge
But it too wanders off among the trees
And peters out. Now it is really dark,
And you have to admit you're lost, lost in the woods.
The dark is alive: it hums and crawls and watches.
You are surrounded by something extremely old
And very clearly have no business here,
Pierced by the sight-lines of a thousand eyes.
You remember all the weird stories you've heard
Of hikers who got lost around these parts,
The hippie couple on their honeymoon,
The scout who wandered from his troop, the hunter
Boastful of plans to track the local lion,
The eccentric traveler who carried bagpipes.
The wood maintains its silence on them all,
As on all those who came with the idea
That nature mirrors the best parts of us,
Inspires and elevates the human soul,
But found, in the end, whatever else they found,
Something indifferent, and only true to itself.
Even if one returns from this experience

THE ECCENTRIC TRAVELER

One does so dazed, not so much disillusioned
As seeing all perception as illusion,
Like someone leaving a cave, or like, perhaps,
Someone who dies for a moment, then is revived
By science or a miracle of art,
Or like the young man out in Washington
Camping alone for the first time, a rite
Of passage into manhood, as he saw it,
Who wandered from his camp looking for water
And lost his way in the coniferous forest:
For days he wandered the primeval forest,
Eating peanut shells, then eating nothing,
And heard, again and again, the absolute silence
Of the great emerald trees silently standing
Straight up the sides of the long-standing mountains,
Then heard a raven, hoarse and raucous, caw,
Or, puncturing the air like a machine gun,
The *rat-a-tat, rat-a-tat, rat-a-tat, rat-a-tat-tat*
Of a woodpecker drilling a hollow pine,
And then the sounds would stop, as in a dream,
As on the forest went, and on he went,
Endlessly lost in the unending forest,
And dizzy from hunger, weakening from hunger,
Drifting into delirium he heard
Something that sounded very much like music
Float through the forest, as if the air were music,
Not like the song of the birds, a human music,
Moody, solitary, elegiac,
The keening, ceremonial tones of bagpipes
Crying for something lost, for someone lost,
Then, quickly, flutes encouraging the bagpipes
Into a marching ditty, and followed the music
Past the erroneous turns of the dark forest
And all the way to the Elkhorn Ranger Station,
Where, walking into their camp like an apparition,
He startled a discouraged group of searchers

THE ECCENTRIC TRAVELER

(None of whom played the flute, or carried bagpipes),
Who led him, without music, out of the woods.

AIR LARRY

Larry Walters flew a lawn chair attached to helium balloons to a height of 16,000 feet, into the jet lanes above Los Angeles; he named his craft "Inspiration I."

When the idea came
It seemed, at best, a dicey thing to do:
You rig your vehicle, give it a name,
Straighten a line or two,

Then, confident you've given it your best
If not that it will carry you aloft,
You put it to the test
And it just takes off,

Lifting you over the trees
And up the sky
Easy as you please,
Till soon you are really high,

Your neighborhood, turned miniature, is gone,
And you wonder how,
Up here all alone,
To get the hell down, now

That the transcendental imagination
Has proven it can indeed
Surpass your wildest expectation
And raise you higher than you need

Or want to go,
For now that you are "there"
All you know is how little you know,
And that here in the upper air

It is very cold,
A disenabling extremity
Your clumsy calculations should have foretold,
And, triggering all your anxiety,

AIR LARRY

You hear, then see, roaring across the sky
As dots in the distance streak into form,
The gargantuan craft come cruising by,
Perfectly uniform,

Built for speed and altitude,
So effortless in shattering sound itself
That next to them your vehicle looks crude
And fatally flawed, just like yourself,

Painfully ill-equipped to play the hero,
And actually beginning to freeze to death
At a temperature far below zero
Where the thin air burns each breath,

And you realize you must, not a moment too soon,
Jettison all original intent
And pop your own balloon
To undertake the perilous descent.

DANTE LOST

> Dante the robot was abandoned on his second
> descent into an active Antarctic volcano.

They've sent him in again, and now he's stuck
On a middle level of volcanic hell.
This time, it seems, he's really out of luck.

He's damaged, just how badly they can't tell.
With difficult retrieval and repair
He's not, they think, worth bringing back. Oh well.

The cost of the whole project can't compare
With all it says, this pilgrim of our time
Caught halfway down the steep infernal stair:

Though art and science correspond like rhyme
Through his descent into the flaming pit,
Such truth and beauty isn't worth a dime.

So there he stays, while we go on with it.
Broken down and written off, he'll dent
And rust, and crack, and topple, bit by bit

And byte by byte, and won't know he was sent
Forth on a quest to question what we know
And failed, and thus was lost. We are hell-bent

To plumb the earth for truth, but want to show
We're cost-effective: there's a bottom line
To every scheme, the one we have to toe.

And the point of the aesthetic is too fine
For even critics to consider now.
Just open another mediocre wine

(Given that worth's subjective anyhow,
And, everything being equal, nothing's higher)
And drink a toast to him, since he can't bow,

DANTE LOST

And won't sing solo in the heavenly choir,
And won't feel the volcano lick his frame
Through transmutations of magmatic fire

Till all that's left is someone else's name.

THE END OF DEWITT FINLEY

1

It was a life of sorts, alone on the road.
Out of the landscape, wind-scrubbed, sparse and vast,
Rose the cold lights of the familiar signs:
McDonald's, Mobil, Day's Inn, Taco Bell ...
And miles to Jordan, miles to Rock Springs Pass,
Then down to Busby, up to Tampico,
Over the Tongue, the Powder, the Musselshell,
While here and there huge tombstones, megaliths,
The buttes loomed over the flatlands, high and dry,
The NEXT REST AREA 200 MILES
Across the dusty, empty middle of nowhere.

But even nowhere's somewhere. The rented room,
Cheap, ugly, badly lit and faintly stale,
Meant something, though he couldn't say quite what.
The stucco lamp, the crease in the coverlet,
The flimsy table, the awkward, orange chair,
The crumpled note in the dented wastebasket ...
For just one night, in the history of this room,
Had two people, really in love, been happy here?
The face in the mirror was one he recognized.
And the shaving kit—how long had he had that?

THE END OF DEWITT FINLEY

2

A short cut up an isolated road
In the mountains of Montana, where the truck
Slips off a switchback hairpin, and gets stuck
In shoulder gravel. Night was coming, cold

In the Rockies in November. He'd stay put.
A genuine fuck-up: he'd lose a day,
Haste making waste, as he knew old Floot would say.
When the sun got up in the morning he'd hike out.

The storm rolled from Alaska down the spine
Of the great range, over the Ogilvies,
The Selwyns, Cassians and Monashees,
A flashing flood, fast rising in a shine

On peak and shoulder, stirrup, scree, plateau,
A swirling avatar of arctic wrath
That avalanched the landscape in its path
With mile on mile of foot on foot of snow,

And, blitzing on, scattered its glittering load,
Precipitating crystal shapes and shifts
Whisked into drifting mounds and massive drifts,
And buried a pick-up sitting by a road.

THE END OF DEWITT FINLEY

3

On the third day,
Sun. The world
Was white.

False hills and ridges
Glared, dazzling,
Everywhere.

A single bird,
Then nothing, silence, snow,
A perfect blank.

"Stay with the vehicle":
He knew the rule.
All help was miles

Through bitter six-foot drifts,
And a man will freeze
Faster than he will starve.

At least there was plenty
To drink, but to eat—
Tums, pine straw, nothing ...

A search plane
Scanned the next road over
And flew on.

After a month
He wrote his boss:
"Death here

In another month
Or so, or He sends
Someone to save me.

THE END OF DEWITT FINLEY

He has met my needs
Daily, and I'm alive,
Well and comforted.

I have no control
Over my life. It's all
In His hands."

He prayed, and slept,
And thought. Until
Too weak to write,

He marked the days
Off a calendar:
Fifty-eight, fifty-nine ...

THE END OF DEWITT FINLEY

4

They found the salesman's body the following spring.
Something struck the observers about the scene
Of the man's death: there wasn't the slightest sign
Of struggle, anguish, or delirium,
No broken glass, no torn upholstery.
All seemed composed, contemplative, serene,
As poised as the steady penmanship,
The thoughtful phrasing, of his calm farewell,
His mild acceptance of his lonely end.

It wouldn't be correct to call it fate:
Rescue, in the form of a ploughed road, remained
Throughout a makable hike away. And though
He didn't know this, did he want to know?
He wanted someone to come, that was the point.
Call it foolishness, or call it faith,
The patience to wait in silence for a sign
That life has something like meaning, and that yours
Has something like meaning, meaning that is yours.

This is a story. Some of it is true.
I heard it from an unreliable friend,
Adding, to her omissions, my distortions.
He was a camper salesman, so perhaps
There never was a pick-up truck, and never
A room (that room was real, but somewhere else).
Even the mild profanity in 2
Would probably have been uncharacteristic.
But the words in 3 are his (those I retrieved
From a transcript of the show *All Things Considered*),
And I have kept his name, because it seems
True to his end, given its pun on fin,
As if the name itself described his plight,
At the wit's end, where finally we all are.

THE END OF DEWITT FINLEY

5

"Stay with the vehicle": is that the rule,
All tenors being tenuous and brief?
Accepting it, there's something like relief,
Or would be, if the ending weren't so cruel,

The life so short, the craft so long to learn.
What point, from way out here, in writing back?
Returning something no one cares they lack,
Forgotten ashes in a dusty urn?

But I'm complaining, as we tend to do
Whenever bad times keep on getting worse.
The heart grows heavier, but not the purse.
The silence lengthens between me and you.

One last mistake. Now loss is all we know.
These words will not, without some act of grace,
Find their way out of this forsaken place
Across those miles of unforgiving snow.

III. Signs and Figures

FROST HEAVES

"Harrison loves my country too,
But wants it all made over new."

In a diminished corner of New England,
Between two pummeled spines of the Green Mountains,
You'll find a town and college, Middlebury,
That once were haunts of the poet, Robert Frost.
He's honored ways some dead would find offensive.
Just read the markers on the road to Randolph
Where the new writers come and go like leaves:
You cross the Robert Frost Memorial Bridge
To see, on the Robert Frost Memorial Drive,
The Robert Frost Interpretive Nature Trail,
The Robert Frost Memorial Wayside Area,
And then a crooked stick-sign, with crude letters,
Warning of shocks from shifty weather: FROST HEAVES.

And who could blame you, pseudo-memorialized
So comically in every wrong direction
Like any Vince Lombardi or Joyce Kilmer?
Or should we rather blame that side of you
Who packaged your keen words like maple syrup,
Dripping with smug provinciality,
Sticky with rhyme? As if you never contrived
To warp the ripe world through thin panes of ice,
Or plotted the marshy ground in fours and fives
Crisp to the cut of your long whispering scythe,
Or started the couple arguing on the stairs,
The narrow, clumsy, stoic will defied
By love's white backward gaze of grief at loss
Till call by liquid call the songbirds changed,
Or hid the goblet behind the children's playhouse.

And now it seems you've gotten me lost again
Although I thought I knew these woods by heart:
Splashes of yellow and alizarin,
Pulse of magenta, every fist in flame.
Something coaxes the trees to dress themselves
In the last colors of the alphabet

FROST HEAVES

Then strips them in the nick of the north wind,
Something crisps the trail, ices the bridge,
Encrusts the plaque in the wayside area
And hoists the pavement, buckling it like clay.
Long after your crumbling image is forgotten
(Beside the hero on inauguration day)
Frost will wrestle stone from underneath
And crack our polished, placid surfaces,
Wrenching apart the road we thought we'd taken.

NOT PLAYING POSSUM

I'd seen him scuttling under a parked car
In the oil-stained sidestreet near the auto shop,
Or peering from beneath the juniper bush
That guarded our old weather-peeled bow porch.
Weirdly primeval, but adaptable
To a landscape of unnatural mutation,
Partly because they will eat almost anything,
His kind is famous for a curious ruse
They put on in a paralytic terror:
If cornered, they play at being carrion
And pray that what's discovered them won't eat them,
A ploy not wholly unlike human tricks,
Like pretending one isn't present while the phone
Rings and rings with the call you refuse to answer,
Or quietly ignoring an ugly scene
Out of discretion or plain cowardice,
Or claiming a poem is merely literal.
Even the most absurd of these games works
Only because it mimics a moment of truth,
Absence or absent-mindedness or poems
Anchored by an unavoidable fact,
And when, one brutal week in mid-July,
The city baked in triple-digit heat
Till its cement was blasting like a furnace,
Drying the last greasy puddles that passed
For water among the staggering animals,
The juniper bush emitted a sickening reek,
A fetid signal that soon crossed the street,
It meant, no matter what the old phrase said,
This possum wasn't playing. He was dead.

LOST PUNCTLES

We'd like to think the marks that mark our pauses,
That stop our sentences, and close our clauses,
Are the effects of universal causes,

That need for such a halt in such a place
Extends from tongue to tongue and race to race.
But history reveals a different case:

Even within the annals of the West
The punctles that still serve at our behest
Are few of many—and where are the rest?

Where's *cryphia*, whose sideways C with dot
Would notify the reader of a spot
Where, though the mark was clear, the text was not?

Percontativus, a backward question mark?
Or punctus versus, lurking like a shark
Beneath the line? All lost in scribal dark.

The common virgule hasn't stuck around
And *punctus elevatus* can't be found,
Nor *positura*, nor a dash compound,

And if you tried to start a paragraph
With something called a *pilcrow* or *paraph*
It would be struck without a qualm or laugh.

Each one is now a sad stylistic no-no;
They've gone the way of dinosaur and do-do;
They've left the game;—like Havlicek, and Jo-Jo.

A DIFFERENT BIRD

Out for a walk
In the woods back of what was a farm
Early one winter morning, surprisingly warm,
No wind, a sky like chalk,

I saw, not heard,
On a branch jutting over the trail,
With a scarlet throat, thrown back, and blue-green tail,
What seemed a different bird.

Without a noise,
Scarcely breathing, for minutes I stood
Deep in that silent, timeless world of wood
Hoping to hear his voice,

Thinking so strange
A songbird must by nature sing
An ecstatic carol, unlike anything
I'd heard for pitch and range,

But, still, no sound.
When I approached, he didn't flinch,
He stared (a warbler? an exotic finch?)
And right up close I found

It wasn't a bird
At all, only a man-made thing
Someone had whittled and painted, beak and wing,
And, though it seems absurd,

Decided to stick
Deep in the woods, for someone like me
To happen upon some day, and see, then see,
And laugh at his little trick,

A DIFFERENT BIRD

And feel a bit lost,
As if the whole walk were a dream
Where things are always never what they seem
In winter woods without frost.

Then, on my word,
(It's unbelievable, I know,
And all this happened, or didn't, years ago),
Turning to leave, I heard,

Not loud or long,
But audible through the forest air,
Coming—from outside? inside?—from somewhere,
Playing, a different song.

CATOPTRIC

Holding the mirror up, like any art
That's any art, reflecting back the world
While reflecting on reflecting back the world,
The hall of mirrors' infinite regress
Where more and more things keep becoming less
And less and vanish where they end or start,

Is what the old masters did, more surely than
They studied the infusions of the soul,
Knowing full well that art exacts its toll
On all who make it and on all they make,
Marking the closest images as fake,
Signing its name in corners where it can,

As in his portrait of a turbaned man,
Containing the scripted "Jan van Eyck made me
21 October 1433"
In drop-dead perfect "carving" on the frame,
The master added, playing on his name,
"Als Ich Kan" (Als Eyck Kan): as well as I can.

THE RELIC

From mishap in the King's baker's house
    In Pudding Lane
  It raced like plague or rumor,
Forking in waves the wakened failed to douse,
Finding on Thames Street oil and hemp and booze
    To feed its humor
  And roll its catastrophic train
    Through side street, square and mews,

  And torch St. Magnus' Church to ash
    Before it came
  Scorching the length of the Bridge
And down to the steelyard in a murderous flash
Levelling strata, consuming poverty
    With privilege,
  A "horrid malicious bloody flame
    As far as we could see"

  (Saw Pepys) arcing "in a bow up the hill"
    Into the City
  As houses cracked and tumbled,
Streets jammed with panic, the chaotic spill
Of carts, goods, horses, people jostled and churned
    And fortunes were fumbled
  In flight from ruin without pity
    Or pause, and London burned.

  When calm and citizens returned
    To the charred scene,
  Little was left of St. Paul's
(Where Wycliffe was tried, and Tyndall's Bible burned).
Among all those memorialized, just one,
    Whose madrigals
  Gave way to sermons, the old Dean,
    Stone-shrouded Dr. Donne,

Someone Else's Name

THE RELIC

Survived as monument and sign,
Though singed, intact,
As if a voice should say:
"Lord, prelate, deacon, burgher, concubine
Shall crumble utterly, with king and queen,
And blow away,
But not this word of my contract,
The English Augustine."

AT THE GRAVE OF BURNS

Ah, Burns, what have they done to ye,
Erecting, for the world to see,
A tomb to native vanity!
    It would be hard
To miss the shades of irony
    In this churchyard.

For in among the grim headstones,
Pockmarked and stoic, where the bones
Of busybodies, drunks and drones
    Were once interred,
While someone spoke, in leaden tones,
    A final word,

They've stuck a temple, shining, sleek,
Palladian and pseudo-Greek,
To lord it over all the meek
    And mark the spot,
For eager acolytes to seek,
    Where you're now not.

Attuned to hagiographic ends,
In white relief, the muse descends,
While your rusticity attends
    Behind the plough.
If you could see where your fine friends
    Have put you now—

Under a silly monument
That contradicts what you most meant:
Your gift was never heaven-sent
    But of the earth,
Of labor to just make the rent,
    And death, and birth.

AT THE GRAVE OF BURNS

And no one laughed at vanity,
The face we want the crowd to see,
The lie of what we'd like to be,
   Louder than you.
But now, the unwitting honoree,
   What can you do?

IN THE PROTESTANT CEMETERY IN ROME

"By shadowy wall and history-haunted street
    Those matchless singers lie,"
Guarded by conical sentries, darkly neat
    Against the perfect sky.

One found a quiet corner, across from the tall
    Point of the pyramid,
The other the crowded base of the coarsened wall.
    If all they wrote and did

Seems touched by such difference, consider this:
    The famous words, in context,
Dissolve in a flood of final bitterness
    At the thought of what comes next,

"The Malicious Power of his Enemies"
    Erasing another name
Consigned to the list of anonymities.
    Obsessed only by fame,

He takes revenge, fighting, in death, for life,
    For life-in-death. And time
Did tell, of course, and all the sore heart's strife
    Seem purposeful as rhyme.

As the other felt in his bones, though driven through
    Such tempests of despair
As torment the quest, but what he saw he knew,
    And he saw the brilliant pair

At the heart of the constellation, and heard the song
    Turn on itself and change,
And knew their scattered words would suffer long,
    Turned something rich and strange.

LOOKING FOR THE LAMA

Something catches the corner of the eye,
The darting, from bush to bush, of a small bird,
Script-black against the exfoliations of green,
Or the glance of sunlight angling in reflection
Off the rainwater in a plastic bucket
Left in the yard, years back, by someone else.

It's just a glimpse, seen darkly, but it triggers
A chain of associations, and the mind
Is off and running down synaptic paths
That spark and fire, connecting the colored words,
The syntactic gardens, embellished by the vital,
Luxuriant intertwinings of metaphor.

And then it's gone, that blur of inspiration.
All that's left is an ordinary scene,
Just a back yard, haphazard and overgrown.
But when you come, as you will, to the end of the day,
Relaxing, thinking of nothing, you will remember
That blur, and dream of a poem, dreaming the words

Arrange themselves to ramify suggestion
According to the arts glimpsed long ago
When you were startled at the scene of reading
By what was happening before your eyes,
And your heart sang, and a deep, addictive music
Colored the world for you, and sent you looking.

And you're still troubled by the moods of looking—
Obsessive, anxious, dull and desperate—
Felt by the scholar sifting for the truth
Through moldy documents of old confusion,
Or by the explorer hopeful of the pole
But penned on the insistence of the blizzard,

Or by, perhaps, the party sent to scan
The barren, frozen corners of Tibet

LOOKING FOR THE LAMA

For someone they believe has been reborn,
Who now, though a small child, contains the man
Who in his heart and mind contains the men
Who've been the man, and senses what they knew:

And when they spread the things before the child
His hands went to the ones the last one owned,
The spectacles, the pencil, long since known
And lifted with conviction, as he smiled.

The elders nodded. The next phase of the plan
Was just as hard, and longer. Who could tell
The lessons he'd be learning all too well,
The child now suddenly become the man?

VIEW OF BALTIMORE FROM GREEN MOUNT CEMETERY

    The nineteenth century
Believed the earth almost a paradise.
    Transported by invention, they came to see
        The world as park and promenade
(Long Sunday afternoons, an orange slice
Of sunset, cakes, another spot of tea),
    And smiled on the new world they'd made,
Sculpting the garden, spurning the cockatrice
    "In the spirit of God."

    Far from the charnel house
And the ripe mephitic whiff of the disinterred,
Essence of rot, inviting cur and mouse
    To churchyards crammed to bursting (this came
To a head in Paris, where the worst occurred:
Long-pressured walls collapsed, and, crumbling, thou-
    Sands of grinning stiffs broke through the frame,
Flooding the basements), where graves, without a word,
    Were dug up name by name,

    They thought of death more gently,
Imagining an afterlife of trees
And grassy slopes, long views from elegantly
    Terraced knolls, a green display,
A pastoral rapture, cast in the shape of these
Visions of death as private and content, the
    Beautiful places, here today,
The suburban landscaped garden cemeteries
    Built after Père Lachaise

VIEW OF BALTIMORE FROM GREEN MOUNT CEMETERY

(Established 1804)
Modelled the virtues of the picturesque:
A resting place almost worth dying for,
With avenues and serpentine
Encirclings, where the marble obelisk,
Marking a family plot with room for more,
Is shaded by the eglantine
Or arborvitae, and the air is brisk
And salutary, fine

Spaces to lounge, make love,
Or mourn, to meditate, to read and roam,
And, finally, fine spots to own a grave
(Security beyond the poor),
With names idyllic as the life to come—
Mount Auburn, Hollywood, Harmony Grove,
Laurel Hill and Pleasant Shore,
Graceland and Evergreen and Forest Home,
Green Mount in Baltimore.

Of course the city has
Long since enclosed the cemetery walls:
Outside the street life peddles drugs and ass,
Whole blocks are boarded up, burned out,
And wary children chase deflated balls
On fields of asphalt sown with broken glass.
Who planned the way these streets turned out?
Nobody. Thoughtless squalor spreads and sprawls
Like pulp some hack churned out.

VIEW OF BALTIMORE FROM GREEN MOUNT CEMETERY

    And yet, surrounded by
All this, this place somehow remains intact.
Without what scant protection money can buy,
    The armed guard and the burglar alarm,
You'd think its treasures would have been ransacked,
Yet even the weather-severed details lie
    Untouched, preserved as if by charm.
A chiseled acorn sits, propped, slightly cracked,
    Detached from human harm.

    The grass is freshly mown,
The shrubs and trees are trimmed, the walks are swept,
And row on row of white and weathered stone
    Pays peaceful tribute to the care
With which these acres of repose are kept.
In here it seems the blights that mar the town,
    The siren shrieks, the bus-fumed air,
The pyramids of trash somebody schlepped
    And dumped, simply aren't there.

    The view we've come here for
Is framed by two angels, posted on ornate
Pedestals. The closest reads "C. DORR":
    Its lookout indicates the skies—
You know the pose—and "the kingdom we await."
(He died on my birthday, 1884.)
    Soot stains his underarm, his eyes,
The folds of his robe. The style is out of date,
    "New words in classic guise,"

VIEW OF BALTIMORE FROM GREEN MOUNT CEMETERY

    Perhaps, as Hardy said
Of Swinburne. Stationed a little down the slope,
The farther angel, praying, bows his head
    And blackened face, as if in grief,
As though to counterpoise the other's hope
That all is well and thriving with the dead,
    Clothed in celestial relief
Like a satin tunic with a silken rope.
    Above the trees in leaf,

    Between the angels, rise
The spires and boxes of the sky-line's range,
The glassy pinnacles of enterprise
    Where mortal fortunes turn and dive,
Like seagulls, with the click of an exchange,
While some poor joe keeps track of the supplies
    And signs for stuff from nine to five,
Stuck in a boss-dug rut that just won't change,
    And feels buried alive.

    The canyons of brick and steel
Carve their ambitious cities out of air.
They echo the hook of the siren song, big deal
    With promises of paradise
On earth, visions of green retirement somewhere
Tropical, with drinks and buxom service. Unreal
    To those of us caught in the vise
Of obligation, attending, with some care,
    To the next roll of the dice.

VIEW OF BALTIMORE FROM GREEN MOUNT CEMETERY

  Next to the lowered head
Of the grieving angel, there's a silver nub:
The cupola atop the copper and lead
  Roof of the Maryland State Pen,
A flaking pyramid, over (here's the rub)
Corridors where the old-style manual dead-
  Bolts slam shut on the lives of men
Who hope for nothing worse than prison grub
  For the next five to ten,

  Or twenty-five to life,
If it is life—who would prefer a cage
To a decent grave? Mother, father, wife
  All eaten by the locust time
While it was doing you at every stage
In solitary, writing like a knife
  In script as permanent as rhyme
Across the perishable skin's soft page,
  For real or imagined crime.

  (Draconian, grotesque,
Ringed with tinsel razor wire, the pen
Predates today's blunt granite Romanesque
  Double-winged and buttressed job,
"The oldest in the hemisphere, open
1811," first prisoner to risk
  Incarceration one "Negro Bob,"
Relieved to escape the chain of wretched men,
  The rain, the railing mob.

VIEW OF BALTIMORE FROM GREEN MOUNT CEMETERY

        For prison walls, too, rose
To thoughts of deep seclusion, in the belief
A place of quiet, if not quite repose,
    Might lead the sinner to reform
His inner world, in penitent relief
From public humiliation: the wheelbarrows,
    The blows, each random, vicious form
Of passing abuse, the hellish curse of grief
        That was the previous norm.)

        The cupola is out
Of use these days, the climb to its bird's-eye
View too perilous and roundabout
    (Across a false ceiling, then up
The swinging steps of a cast-iron spir-
Al staircase), but for years the watch looked out
    Over the rowhouse roofs and up
To the outskirts to see, against the sky,
        The place they might end up

        Were they "establishment"
(Which they, of course, were not): the cemetery
Rising like the dream of all it meant
    In silent plotlines on the hill,
With chapel, cross, and steeple, which would bury
All fear of exhumation, of being rent
    Up from what rest the body will
Receive, in pruned arrangements green and airy,
        Manicured and still.

VIEW OF BALTIMORE FROM GREEN MOUNT CEMETERY

  (It's like a painting, and,
If there's a painting, the painter sketches in
And then rubs out a figure, shears in hand,
  Who labors in the midday heat,
A black groundskeeper. Now he goes back in
Against the white tombstones, where he will stand
  For other labor, other sweat,
Before the work—O why did we begin?—
  Is finally complete.)

  So here is where hereafter
Starts, or ends, on the far side of this grass
That covers sorrow as it covers laughter.
Locus amoenus, haven, garden, bower,
Bliss is illusion, yes, where all things pass.
The statuary whispers what comes after
  Only when we're gone. The hour
Is late, that much we know, as window glass
  Catches a sun sunk lower,

  Making it very clear
It's time to go. All that's left to be done
Is nod to what remains of sleepers here,
  Including my cousins Symington
And a poet of some distinction, Sidney Lanier,
Under a massive, pink-veined riverstone
  Ever since 1881,
Bearing a plaque with final words, his own:
  "I am lit with the sun."

PEREGRINE FALCON ON SKYSCRAPER

At home on ledges
High up a granite scarp,
Accustomed to the view
From cutting edges

Of thrust, abutment,
Rock on rock, and sharp
Extensions into blue
Air's element,

Through which she will,
From far above the trees,
Tuck in her wings and drop
To stick the kill,

Or, turning, ride
The spirals of a breeze
All the way to the top,
Then dip to glide

Back down the sheer
Vectors and fractals that
Compose the swirling eddies
Of atmosphere,

And all the time
A feathered acrobat
Who's utterly at ease
With the sublime

Of mountain range
And sunset's cameo,
The cloud-stacked ceiling sprung
By waves of change,

PEREGRINE FALCON ON SKYSCRAPER

    The peregrine
Or "pilgrim falcon" (so
Named because, when young,
    She's captured in

    "Pilgrimage,"
Or passage from the nest,
Being most highly prized,
    For pure courage

    And deadly speed,
As all in all the best
Hunter, though undersized,
    Of any breed,

    Thus widely sought
By the keen falconer
Who's caught the gaming itch,
    Who'll have her taught,

    By hood and blind,
Sharp hunger, jess and lure
And whistle, to rise to pitch,
    Then stoop and bind

    The flushed, stunned quarry—
Blackbird, partridge, pheasant,
Lark, crow, rook, quail, gull, teal—
    And not to carry),

    True to her name,
Has passed into the present
Landscape of brick and steel,
    Taking what came

PEREGRINE FALCON ON SKYSCRAPER

    As habitat
And vantage point on all
Within the telescope
    Of eyesight that

    Sees everything
That moves, however small,
And, far beyond our hope
    That anything

    So natural
And fierce could find its way
Within the maze we've made
    Out of it all

    (The world she knew
For eons if a day,
Decked out in every shade
    Of green and blue,

    Dusky and clear
Millenia and more,
The artful, self-rebuilding
    Old biosphere),

    Has come to nest
Outside the thirteenth floor
Of the Legg Mason building,
    And faces west

    To watch the sun
Light up the toxic haze
Our factories emit,
    Or lifts to run

PEREGRINE FALCON ON SKYSCRAPER

And float and dive,
Adapting to these days
With speed and heart and wit
  That will survive.

CHECKERED PRESENT

1

Projects of a dubious nature were undertaken
And went awry, leaving his friends in jail.
He hung around, shady, telling a tale
Less than convincing and, now, clearly shaken.

2

It was the single thing she wanted to see
The first thing every morning (she was three)—
 The blooming bow, the "black-white" wrapping paper—
Camilla's biggest present under the tree.

3

The times are spotty, and just getting worse,
Black squares vs. red squares, you vs. me.
What moves of interest won't we want to see
While living out the ancient Chinese curse?

4

And now the boy always wanted to play,
Though you grew tired of this, as did your rump.
But he was thrilled by every triple jump,
Triumphant in his world another day.

5

The basic contrast serves at any age
As space fills up with letters, as in Scrabble,
Be it central wisdom, be it babble,
The chiaroscuro of the scribbled page.

CHECKERED PRESENT

6

But now the copula's in ill repute,
The myth of presence being something past.
The signifier stumbles, coming last.
It's lame, its dog don't hunt, its gun won't shoot.

7

The sword slid from the niche where it was wedged
But now all bets are off or, at best, hedged.
    Words slice back through the handler in a flash.
The gift is nothing if not double-edged.

8

And every present has designs on you,
Dear reader. I do hope you've had some fun
Unwrapping the layers of this crisscrossed pun.
What's inside is, well, absent. I am too.

WORDS ON WORDS

He opened the largest book, and here they came,
The frank, the angled, and the hammered latten
Of ceremonial vessels, all in rows,
Quicksilver, paid on both sides, implicated,
Astral, claustral, crystal, murky, crossed
Out or floated forth, rigged like a flight
Of fancy calculation, riding the waves
Of dream and trauma, thrill and desperation
(O, let her see!), at sea on the letter C,
And all for love of something in the mirror,
Not you, the curve of the world, all color and sky,
Sunlight and fenestration opening on Rome,
To be referred to, "signpost," in this language
They are, and it must change, and they must change,
Captured by science, context or confusion,
Parameters turning perimeters in a fog,
But calling out, always, to all they would name,
The sign/thing sine curve thing, like thing and sign
Were thing and wave at once, a cursive sign
Written on water by wind with fire from earth
In the richest contradictions of connotation,
Doing a triple back flip telling a joke
On up through inside under over and out.

YOUNG WILL SHAKESPEARE

Henry VI Part I

Enter, raving, the demonic Joan of Arc:
O kill her for the glory of bloody England!

Two Gentlemen of Verona

Well, see, there's these two guys, and they're just jerks,
But the beautiful women fall for them anyway.

Henry VI Part II

Now chronicle the times when blackened skies
Etc.

Henry VI Part III

And finally the villain of the piece
Begins to show his singular, evil self,
Bitterly deformed, and, like the play, all plot.

Richard III

So entertainment sells itself to all
Though warts are visible, and crooked smiles
Repulse only to lure you, leering, in.
The shadow of an enormous caricature
Falls on the audience, a final rant
Rings up applause as coffers chime "full house."

YOUNG WILL SHAKESPEARE

Titus Andronicus

Yeah, sure, your style's a rip-off, and your plots
Are bits and pieces, or borrowed whole—who cares?
The game's a game. Just take it over the top.
Want horrors? Want to be shocked and thrilled? Grossed out?
Well here she is, our lovely amputee,
Just ravaged by those villains out of Marlowe.

King John

He soon hates almost all he's done, of course,
The limits of stick-figure melodramas,
Cluttered with queens on tirade, suddenly clear.
(He's being mocked for just such stuff right now.)
Where is the human, real against history?
Left off the rolls, another bastard, poor,
Yes, but with features hinting at something regal.
He's any man spat on and pigeonholed
Until he's had it, damned straight he's a player,
And he'll walk right into history if he pleases.

The Taming of the Shrew

So what's a play? Illusion that becomes,
True paradox, more real than "life itself,"
Reflecting back our passionate roles cast large?
(Or trying: the audience, a drunken dullard,
Snoozes, drooling, dreaming of sex and luxury.)
What's real is a world where women are property.
But life's a play, so gender roles are roles.
In asking for your hand, if I propound,
In most ridiculous garb, bald idiocies
Puffed up by the flimsiest patriarchal whimsy,
Perhaps you'll humor my folly and play along

And we can use this knowledge to advantage.
Such irony is freedom, in life as art.

The Comedy of Errors

There's triple trouble when the doubling trope
Quadruples the confusion, and Classic Text,
A stooped old man, is slated for execution
By a limber upstart fighting with hands and feet.
The crowds, the jugglers, the conjurors, the warnings
Of the apostle blur and morph, a dark
Conceit deflected to something farcical,
A mask where we are who they say we are.
(And not, of course, without a nod to commerce,
The lawyers leaping on tables and shouting for more.)
So the old tale's made new, and the old mother,
Remembering each error, trumps the law.

MOBILE BAY JUBILEE

On a calm night, in summer or early fall,
Along the eastern shore of Mobile Bay
(Just where and when, no one can truly say:
The tales told here are honest, even when tall),
    The bay is glass, and all
That moves is just enough soft breeze to lay
The surface water down as if asleep,
The tide crawls in, and in a hypnotic way
Up to the shore miraculously creep
    Small creatures of the deep,
Catfish and shellfish, flounder, eels, and rays,
Thronging the shallows, floundering in a daze,
All the fresh seafood you can eat, for free,
There to be picked and cooked your favorite ways,
    The bounty of jubilee
    When the fish come forth from the sea
And the sweet flesh of the deep can be had for a song
Until the tide runs out, which is not long.

An hour or two, typically, sometimes more,
Agree the experts, all from "right 'round here,"
The twelve-mile stretch from Daphne to Point Clear
Where tales of plenty are the local lore,
    Who sit, scanning the shore
Past midnight in the dog days every year,
Watching the bay give back the tall night sky,
Hoping to see the first few eels appear,
The sign of more to come, and fish to fry,
    And then up goes the cry
"Jubilee! Jubilee!" and now the people come,
With buckets and nets and gigs, from car and home,
In flushed, frenetic spontaneity,
A dance of flounder lights, shuffling through foam
    For the bounty of jubilee
    When the fish come forth from the sea
And the sweet flesh of the deep can be had for a song
Until the tide runs out, which is not long.

MOBILE BAY JUBILEE

Scenes of vast harvest, acts of staggering greed!
Two hundred flounder speared, or three, or six
(The concupiscent get themselves into a fix:
Mountains of fish to clean, they'll rue the deed
    As a gigged foot will bleed
From an eager, errant jab that hits and sticks—
A jubilee's hard work, and does get gory);
Or reaping hoards of stunned crabs, that affix
Themselves to bayside logs and the odd dory ...
    It seems a big fish story
Of unbelievable luck out of the blue,
Rank with exaggeration the whole way through,
Beyond the arc of possibility
In daily life or art, except it's true
    To the bounty of jubilee
    When the fish come forth from the sea
And the sweet flesh of the deep can be had for a song
Until the tide runs out, which is not long.

For there are scientific explanations
(Though these, like stories, tend to multiply:
What happens happens, then we stab at why)
Of these "sporadic mass shoreward migrations
    Of demersal fish and crustaceans":
The ratio that prevails, fall to July,
Of fresh to salty water in the bay,
Changes as summer lengthens; if tide's high,
And certain wind conditions are in play,
    The fresh water gives way,
Salinity increasing more and more,
To bottom-water, heavy, oxygen-poor,
Till, used to better breathing, the fish flee
Ahead of the salty water, to the shore,
    Thus causing a "jubilee"
    When the fish come forth from the sea
And the sweet flesh of the deep can be had for a song
Until the tide runs out, which is not long.

MOBILE BAY JUBILEE

This does explain the fishes' odd behavior,
The way they flop and wobble and gulp air
In search of energy from anywhere,
Till sunrise or tide shift serves as savior
    And out they swim, a wave your
Exhausted jubileers scarcely care
To see take form and ripple and recede:
They've caught plenty to eat, with more to share,
However many mouths they have to feed,
    With anyone in need,
And planned to spread their fortune when they took
More than they intended to clean and cook,
Though most do have a favorite recipe
(Many are in *The Jubilee Recipe Book*)
    For after a jubilee
    When the fish come forth from the sea
And the sweet flesh of the deep can be had for a song
Until the tide runs out, which is not long.

A few of these are: Curried Shrimp Supreme,
Shrimp Jambalaya, Devilled Crabmeat Mold
(A little tricky to make, and best served cold),
Crab Stuffed Potatoes, Flounder in Sour Cream,
    Every Fisherman's Dream
(A mushroom, tomato, and seafood casserole),
Shrimp Ramekens, Baked Flounder Florentine,
Crabmeat in Avocado, Shrimp Creole
For Twenty-five, Beer Shrimp, Crab Amandine,
    Flounder Sautéed in Green
Sauce, Very Heavenly Flounder (lightly oiled,
Then grilled in bacon), French Fried Shrimp, Shrimp Boiled
In Ice Cream Salt, Whole Flounder Stuffed with Brie,
And on and on, deep-fried and baked and broiled
    Dishes for jubilee
    When the fish come forth from the sea
And the sweet flesh of the deep can be had for a song
Until the tide runs out, which is not long.

MOBILE BAY JUBILEE

It's fitting that the sagging table fills
With gifts from water, where the maps are lined
With rivers: Alabama is defined
By fluvial arteries running off its hills
    To merge in one that spills,
Splintering to alluvial, intertwined
Bayous, into the bay. As someone who's a
Reader of maps will tell you, you will find
The Alabama forming where the Coosa
    Joins with the Tallapoosa
Beyond Eclectic, then squiggling its way west
To add the Cahaba to its seaward quest,
Then south to meet the Tombigbee (not the Pea)
And branch and fan into the bay that's blessed
    By the bounty of jubilee
    When the fish come forth from the sea
And the sweet flesh of the deep can be had for a song
Until the tide runs out, which is not long.

And fitting, too, that the most musical names
Are native names, for the voice that we keep hearing
In "Alabama" (Choctaw: "I make a clearing")
Is all that's left (one of our two great shames,
    Whatever we say in games),
With scraps, of a life forever disappearing:
Arrowhead, moccasin, chipped earthenware,
A stone plug that was worn as a kind of earring ...
When land was spirit, moving everywhere,
    They heard, drilling the air,
The woodpecker's beak attacking a hollow core,
And spotted the shadowed deer on the forest floor,
And, stunned by their fortune, were the first to see
The dazed, unlucky fish come reeling ashore,
    The original jubilee
    When the fish came forth from the sea
And the sweet flesh of the deep could be had for a song
Until the tide ran out, which was not long.

MOBILE BAY JUBILEE

Today's landscape is scribbled with other names:
Jubilee Carwash, where a huge plastic crab
Steps awkwardly over a little pre-fab
Gas station (Texaco); or neon proclaims
    Jubilee Video Games;
Jubilee Music is scrawled on the glass of a drab
Storefront, next to a shrimp on saxophone;
And Jubilee Parkway, Jubilee Photo Lab,
Jubilee Landscaping, Jubilee Savings and Loan ...
    We take things for our own,
And the term itself has come to represent
Our festive response, and not the real event
Now prized for its marketability,
The prodigal and seemingly heaven-sent
    Natural jubilee
    When the fish come forth from the sea
And the sweet flesh of the deep can be had for a song
Until the tide runs out, which is not long.

Is this a further sign of usurpation,
Like the deforestation of the land,
Pollutions calculated and unplanned,
The murderous, self-righteous dislocation
    Of every native nation
By compulsion to supply each new demand?
Or would that press the argument past call?
This clumsy taking of what comes to hand
Seems, rather, genial and comical,
    No figure for our fall,
But indicative of something that survives
Even in our contemporary lives,
An innocent, exuberant jollity
Which animates the spirit as it thrives
    In the moment of jubilee
    When the fish come forth from the sea
And the sweet flesh of the deep can be had for a song
Until the tide runs out, which is not long.

MOBILE BAY JUBILEE

It's cause for celebration, then, this feast
Of plenty, inspiration for any cook,
A miracle, like a story in a book
About a prophet (ask the nearest priest—
    He'll tell you two, at least)
Whose powers so frightened Simon that he shook:
When he'd caught nothing on Gennesaret
The master bid him cast, and that cast took
So many fishes that it broke his net;
    Who later, better yet,
Turned two fish and five barley loaves to food
To feed, with baskets left, a multitude
In the hills beside the waters of Galilee,
And "lest they faint in the way" sent them forth renewed
    From a feast like a jubilee
    When the fish come forth from the sea
And the sweet flesh of the deep can be had for a song
Until the tide runs out, which is not long,

Or like a theme we might go forth to find
At play within a world without a map,
Surfacing on a walk, or in a nap,
The music of whatever comes to mind,
    Scored in a form designed,
Like a baroque, demented booby trap,
To catch its victim, reader, by surprise
When whittled points of slant connection snap
In place, resembling, to attendant eyes,
    A figuring that lies
In and about all correspondent things.
Words float in their formations as on wings,
In search of something, sentient and free,
Arriving on the breeze that turns and sings
    A chant like a jubilee
    When the fish come forth from the sea
And the sweet flesh of the deep can be had for a song
Until the time runs out, which is not long.

IDENTITY THEFT

for Carla

I. Trajectories

THE CATCH

Scientists recently announced that huge Asian big head carp are on their way to the Great Lakes. The fish are known for jumping into fishermen's boats, often causing injury. — *The Washington Post*

After some twenty-odd years
    In dubious boats
    ("You call *that* a craft?")
("Well, sometimes it kind of floats"),

With hand-me-down, broken tackle,
    Vanishing bait,
    And a boredom only
Sleep can alleviate,

As patience keeps coming up empty
    Like a snapped line
    ("Though this is all
I have, it isn't mine"),

When fish are merely theory
    And hunger a fact,
    And not a thing
Worth eating gets caught in the act

But the odd compliment,
    Not what you fish for,
    Till wishing your wishing
Would end is all you wish for,

Out of the blue comes news
    Of aquatic confusion
    And piscatory
Peril from the intrusion

Into our longest rivers
    And largest lakes,
    Occasioning
Slack jaws and double takes,

Identity Theft | 117

THE CATCH

Plus bruises, cuts, and pains
    Both dull and sharp,
    Of strange, colossal
Asian big head carp

That grow to sixty pounds
    And four feet plus,
    And as if impelled
By compulsion to concuss

Jump ten feet in the air
    And, willy-nilly,
    Crash land in boats,
Knocking the fishermen silly,

As if we weren't so already,
    Setting out
    In quest of triumphs
Brief as a waterspout

And rarely as substantial,
    Often consisting
    Of great improbable
Trophies we keep insisting

We actually almost landed
    One fine day
    (The luring headline:
HUGE FISH GETS AWAY),

Until such whoppers seem
    The whole intent
    Of annals of
Piscine endeavorment

THE CATCH

And we drift, careless, breezy
   ("What's that bumpin'?")
   ("Maybe a big one,
Eh? Let's hope they're jumpin'") ...

Better reel in the line
   And batten the hatch.
   You finally got
What you asked for. That's the catch.

IDENTITY THEFT

The perils of our hyperdigital age
Hover in microrealms of cyberspace,
Waiting to disappear the vanished page
(What brief felicities fell out of place,
What midnight labors lost to lose the case!)
You (expletive!) *deleted,* zapped to square
Zero, cut past retrieval, launched into space
Blacker than black holes, thinner than thin air,
A technoillogic anti-world that isn't there.

Now all our information circulates
Through networks, camouflaged and limacine,
That monitor accounts and payment dates
And know just what we've bought, know where we've "been,"
And sell that information, site unseen,
To anyone pretending enterprise.
We're just a set of numbers on a screen,
Numbers that serve the purposes of lies
Inducing massive information compromise.

Some sly, pretexting phisher, who's expert
In legerdemain's most current digital cons
To siphon funds before a fraud alert,
Brandishes false security icons
And, deft as a neurosurgeon slicing pons,
Breaches our firewall, accessing our cache.
His toxic terms invade our lexicons,
Taxing our systems staggering toward a crash
But not before he's flowed our info into cash.

It seems that someone else has got your name
Where all identity is virtual
And masquerade is party to the game,
And as he plays your credit's in free fall.
The world his oyster, the false You's having a ball
In Punta Cana, Mexico, Brazil.
Where all is credit, some will credit all:

IDENTITY THEFT

Aiming at your good name, with time to kill,
He's scripting your only move, he's virtually writing your will.

But who needed that identity, anyway?
Your very number's socially insecure,
And daily, faceless at the NSA
Behind black glass, empowered to secure
Security, they're spying, that's for sure,
Safe in their cubical polyopticon,
With satellite interception to insure
They're on our chatter as we chatter on,
All processed by the secret program Echelon.

So so long privacy, and any sense
Identity itself remains intact.
There's no such thing as virtual innocence.
Now everything's public, every public act
Is you, you're John Q. Public, since in fact
You line up like the next guy, you're just the same,
Same suit, same shoes, exactly the same contract,
The social one of inquisition, shame,
And punishment by numbers, lots. What's in a name?

(And your own name was always your father's, too,
The first you, and the bigger man as well,
Which made you number two, the second you.)
Names do have their intentions, they bluntly tell
Too little or too much. If Florimell—
No, let her wait. Say that your folks, in pride,
Decided Abraham Lincoln Graham Bell
Might augur greatness ... Their friends were horrified,
The future much amused, and you, you wanted to hide.

For what's more arbitrary than a name?
Even "identity," that seminal term,
Derives from "*idem,*" which just means "the same."
But same as what? As whom? Confused, infirm,

IDENTITY THEFT

The sense of self as core, essential germ
Emerging from the vast genetic scrum
Through coded interplay of egg and sperm
As someone really you, is overcome,
Cleaned up, sponged off, wiped out, stopped *in exordium*.

Identity itself becomes the thief
Stealing away with all we never had.
We've changed? Matured? Turned over a new leaf
In the volume of the self? Or slipped? Gone bad?
The epic of our lives, the ___ *iad*,
Has no one in it stable enough to change,
Whether the hero's Artegall or Chad:
No growth potential, no peak, no depth, no range.
It's all far too familiar, and then it's all too strange.

The person in the mirror isn't me,
He isn't anyone. Image is all
Or nothing. Now reality TV
Becomes our window on the world, the fall
Brings brand old characters, in what we call
Interesting situations: tension, strife,
Treachery, eating insects. It's comical,
Or would be if the spectacle weren't rife
With resonant hollowness, our need to get a life.

But if we had a life, what would we do?
There's freedom in not being anyone.
Pronominal confusion—"me" and "you,"
Like "us" and "them," are codependent, "one"
Must, nervous, glance at "many," as the son
Looks backward at the father—runs amok.
Though you *were* one of us, under the gun
We've joined them, and you are out of luck.
When asked our name (whose name?) in court, you stood, dumbstruck.

IDENTITY THEFT

And what identity you have you stole.
That smile, that gesture, that quirky turn of phrase
Are just as patterned as the caracole
The rider learns to manage. All your days
You've been accumulating such displays
Of influence. It's easy enough to date
The habits of your practice, phase by phase.
You're hybrid, mongrel, patchwork, complicate,
A gallimaufry. Just be yourself? It's far too late.

You're no more you than you're a character
Lost in the labyrinth of *The Faerie Queene*.
"This path leads where? Why are there two of her?"
You've double Florimells to choose between:
The differences are huge, but can't be seen.
It's all a hall of mirrors, with no way out,
Endless. You multiply. Behind the screen,
Immeritô, E. K., and Colin Clout
Masked and unmasked, identity remains in doubt.

Scholars are fools by trade, but so's the poet
Whose narcissistic tale, which he must tell,
Rings full of echoes and he doesn't know it.
In seeking who you are, you might as well
Be one of the knights pursuing Florimell
Who, scared of everything, keeps running away,
Streaking by on her palfrey like a bat out of hell.
(The true one, that is; the false one's glad to stay.)
No, you can't win the game, and, yes, you have to play.

And Florimell's girdle, apogee of art
And echoing renown, self without end?
All the Old Masters have a big head start
And who are you? To what do *you* pretend?
Fasten your armor, chump, prepare to defend
Yourself against the champion, The Past.
Under enormous pressure you will bend

IDENTITY THEFT

Then snap. The game will play you, hard and fast,
From your first tentative misstep to your tottering last.

Retired, you're shipped off to the Last Resort
Where the old losers linger, contemplating
What might have been. There's never a final report,
Just a slow, blurry fade-out, with everyone waiting
For nothing to stop happening. False You's dating
False Florimell, but no one heard the chimes
At midnight, once. Abe Lincoln Bell's berating
His cell phone; Artegall's up on war crimes;
Chad should be, too. Oh well. These are, or were, bad times.

Or you wander, at last, into the Cave of Despair,
The site the evil omens all portend:
The scattered corpses, the cries, the putrid air,
The smooth-talking assassin who's your friend.
You've broken more than you can ever mend
And debts are never cancelled. What's up? The game.
You know who's coming to get you in the end,
The ultimate thief who takes us all the same
And pockets every precious asset, even your name.

VIRTUAL DEATH

A Korean man collapsed and died after playing a video game for 49 hours straight. It was one of several similar deaths over the last few years.

Let's not pretend we don't know how he felt,
The compulsion of obsession, pushing beyond
The limits of the body, because the mind,
Synapses firing and firing, can't let go.
The body's nothing, weak, its miserable needs—
A shift in posture, sleep, a little food—
Are nothing compared to adrenal presences
Like fear and joy unleashing their jolts, and now
You're hooked on this one, figuring the terrain,
Marking the dangers, starting to read the game,
And, yes, invested in your character
Whose life or death is really on the line
And matters, more than you know or want to know.

(The game is Starcraft, battle simulation
With multiplayer mayhem on the edge
Of the galaxy, intuitive interface
With hard-core gamers hundreds of miles away
Camped in the cybercafes and jacked to the skies,
Living on instant noodles and cigarettes,
Napping on fold-out cots, then back to action
Wired up, dialed in, locked on, and wary of movement:
Protoss, Zergs, and Terrans are on the prowl
As cracks in the Alliance begin to spread,
Dark Templars start appearing—what's *their* motive?—
And all beware Kerrigan, Queen of Blades ...)

A life on-line—with whose life on the line?
Somewhere a clock ticks, pressure takes its toll,
The body paying with every vital amp
Firing away. Let's not pretend, late night,
Light-headed, eyes fixed on the morphing screen
So long past quitting time time seems to stop,
When space shrinks to an artificial window
Where every swerve brings peril, joy, and fear

VIRTUAL DEATH

And on you battle, missing the hidden turn
Out of the labyrinth, missing the word
Sharp as a Saxon sword to slay the beast
Still howling for sacrifice, let's not pretend
We don't know how he felt, unable to stop.

Not even when a worried emissary
From your frantic mother reaches the cybercafe
Pleading with you to come home, get some rest,
Some decent food: but now the game is peaking,
In a blaze of spectral fire you live or die
And terminate your epic compulsive quest,
You've played the game, it's played you, and you're done,
You stagger to the bathroom, collapse on the floor
("Heart failure from exhaustion"), and really die
Where space is virtual but time is time.

HIKIKOMORI

Japanese for "withdrawal," the term refers both to the condition of those people, usually young males, who retreat to their room and refuse to come out, sometimes for many years, and to those suffering from that condition, estimated by at least one expert to constitute 1% of the Japanese population.

Though the phenomenon is Japanese,
The impulse, to do precisely as you please,
Turning your back on social expectation,
Parental pressure, class humiliation,
And all the rapid brutal give and take,
More take than give both on and off the make,
Of going to and fro, from habit or need,
In this our world ramped up to hyperspeed
And taxing every jumpy nerve we've got
With information surfeit, polyglot
Configurations of whatever next
Installment of the social hypertext
Is paramount lest one be left behind
The swift proverbial curve and flounder, mind
Out of time times out of mind, is common to
The species. Since the whole thing's coming to
An interfacing universal mess
To end all messes in a vast distress
So intercalibrated we will all
Fall in a nanosecond of one fall
By someone lapsing somewhere (a butterfly's wings
Set off a chain reaction, and all things
Sink to sheer ruin and sudden misery,
As melting ice caps slide into the sea),
The social contract doesn't look so great.
You didn't want this. Why participate?
In cultures where there's nothing but the norm
And confident assumption you'll conform,
Without resort to clubs and cliques and clans
Like gangs and Goths and Young Republicans
To band together in an anti-style
Or posse up and angrily revile
The Bloods or Democrats, ready to do

Identity Theft | 127

HIKIKOMORI

One in, without such dark companions, you
Are nothing but yourself. What need for more
Mutual disappointment? Shut the door.
Though now your world is cramped, dank, minuscule,
It has one denizen who has one rule:
Do what you want with your own precious time.
And there are moments, bordering on sublime
(Though these do grow less frequent, year by year)
When mind unlocks its vistas, and the sheer
Infinitude of possible combinations
That ramify in endless implications
Just opens up, and suddenly you see,
Like a man on top of a mountain near the sea.
And though these overwhelm, leaving you dizzy,
Weak-kneed, disoriented, peaked (physi-
Ologically, your lifestyle, so to speak,
Is less than ideal: every other week,
Past midnight, you sneak out to an all-night store,
Fluorescent and deserted, to get some more
Potato chips, Sprite, Ramen, frozen meals,
And cigarettes), until the whole room reels,
You tell yourself it's worth it. And you tell
Yourself, "I could be bounded in a nutshell
And count myself the king of infinite space,"
Or simply count yourself. That's one. In place
Of everyone you have yourself to blame
For all or nothing. You barely know your name
And barely need to. You failed at something, long
Ago, you think, though who was right or wrong
Matters less and less in the blur of years
Since you took cover, shutting out your fears.
Nothing gets through that door you live behind
Where the whole world is what you have in mind.

TRAJECTORY

Who were we, back before the whole world changed?
The person jabbering in the street alone
    Was certainly deranged.
      Now he's just on the phone.
  Perhaps he's trading futures—but with whom?
Can I trade mine? Or ours? But I'm a pod,
    My palm is piloted.
Have we been saved, or Pontius Pilated?
What else beside our numbers got exchanged,
    What records pirated?
    What happened to our safety zone?
    Where there's great reckoning
        There's little room,
        Even for odd.
With all the shining dials set on zoom,
    What fave new world is beckoning?
      What artificial god
With mega-memory, who does not nod?

I can't not go along. Lord knows I've tried
To keep myself from getting up to speed
    On this text-messaged ride.
      In word, if not, indeed,
In correspondence, then at least in verse,
I've felt the antiquated urge to try. Way
    Back before we let
Happen the things that hadn't happened yet,
Who thought we'd choose vehicular suicide?
    And now, caught in the net,
    Attached, we tell ourselves we're freed.
    The crashes we don't mention.
      There's no reverse,
      No hidden byway.
Will we be masters of the universe,
    Grand techno-wizards, *Übermenschen*
      Singing "I Did It My Way"?
Or roadkill on the information highway?

THE LAST BOOK

Such things were treasured objects, long ago,
Bound in calf's leather, framed by marbled boards,
Arranged by code in capitals, prized hoards
Of variorum, quire, and folio.

But now, downloaded, Xeroxed, put on tape
To quicken the commute's redundant trip,
Whole *oeuvres* shrink onto a microchip
And, volume after volume, lose their shape.

Who'll be the very last human to hold
One of these curious relics in his hands,
And think of vanished rivers, vanished birds,

And wonder why, in distant times and lands,
We made such settings for the tales we told
And placed such binding value on our words?

II. Odes and Elegies

ELEGY

Another year is done
And still you're gone.

ODE

O elevated visionary thoughts,
Where are you now?

FOR A SEASON

Somehow the pieces clicked at the right time,
Triumph fed triumph, and we won it all.
We were the state-of-the-art invincible
Until the fall. And did we fall.

FOR THE OLD WOMEN

Where are they gone, the old women bent double,
The ancient woman across the alley, who tended
The peach tree, a huge wool hat in all weathers
At a right angle? Or the muddled old crone
Next door, frail but persistent, who kept stealing
My garbage cans, thinking I was throwing them out?

Under the earth like an old mother.

TO FALSE SPRING

You've tricked the flowers out
   So now they die.

These are the signs
Of deity as premature arrival,
   These are the lies.

ON A PORCELAIN BOWL

Faux Oriental blue, your figures faded,
Your legend blurred (what ritual?), and still
You're warm with what's been kept in you (coins, pins).
Surely there's truth in that. (And beauty, too.)

TO A HOUSE SPARROW

Drab avatar of all that's ordinary,
Dull-uniformed, monotonous in song
    (If it *is* song),
Low-flying, mostly hopping along the ground,
You're not immortal or incomparable
But still my heart aches in a minor key
    For what you are.

ON LETHARGY

Too tired to write, to read, to anything!
Prisoners of heat indices, we drowse.
The chair is easy, leaving it is hard
And naps in sequence like the Florida Keys
Stretch off across the summer ...

Love, ambition, poetry ask so much
And we are so sleepy ...

FOR AN APPLE TREE

The landlord's murdered you. Your trunk's been bored,
Riddled with holes for poison, and now your leaves
Are brown as dust in August. Dying in summer!
Your apples were inedible in abundance.

The birds and squirrels won't come here anymore.

That you live on in my poems is no consolation.

TO THE WIND

Lift all the summer's green epiphanies,
Yellowed to rust and fire,
And blow them away
O Arctic, O Canadian,
Scurry them into troughs for the underworld!

INTIMATIONS

Consider why
As infants, left alone
We cry and cry,
Straining our brand new cords
As if our hovering parents were really gone.
Surely we bawl
Under the awful stress
Of terror more primal than words,
Where absence is nothingness
And presence is all.

The constellation
Of the mobile above my crib
In circulation
Seemed the perpetual sway,
As shapes and colors would twirl and dip and jib,
Of amniotic motion.
But when it stopped
All comfort was snatched away,
As if I'd been casually dropped
In a freezing ocean.

If we could see
In a mirror the wrinkled face
Of infancy,
Would we half-recognize
In bewildered creases and furrows the frightened trace
Of an old, old man?
What in heaven had we been through?
Though we were never wise,
Was there something huge we knew
For a brief span?

Our vertigo
Does, quietly, dissipate
As we cease to know
The abyss of our becoming.

Identity Theft

INTIMATIONS

Words turn the world to a tale we learn to relate,
    But that's a stage.
We mumble along in error
    Forgetting what's coming,
Return to original terror
    Like a blank page.

FOR DONALD JUSTICE

(1925–2004)

The years have failed us, as you knew they would.
Your eyes have closed at last, like the great storm shutters
On the grand hotels that only you remembered,

And as Florida gets hammered coast to coast
After the tragic season of your death
("Great Leo roared"), there isn't any justice.

(You'd wince at that, I think; I know you would.)

O memories of shadows, sunken porches,
Arcades, piano lessons, and the frail
Attempts to practice culture in the suburbs,

O hints of juniper, mysterious scents,
And the soft gradual darkening of chords
That somehow summons up the Great Depression

(Those subtleties my parents would remember
Were they alive—sometimes when reading you
I almost feel I'm hearing *them* remember),

Who will recall you now? There are no more words.

FOR ANTHONY HECHT

(1923-2004)

All style and substance, elegant and grave,
Versed in the courts of wit, and the stark places
    Sought by the wounded mind,
The heart's chambers of love, and atrocity's cave,
You put us younger poets through our paces
    With terms both strict and kind,

And, teaching by example, showed us how,
In terpsichorean stanzas learned by heart
    And smooth as alabaster,
To make the ancient forms sing here and now
With *sprezzatura*'s poise concealing art
    That earned the title "master."

Can one so measured when he took the floor
With death itself, and danced that sarabande
    With breath-taking aplomb
At tempi fitted to the chilling score,
Really have stopped? The quartet halts, unmanned.
    The instruments are dumb.

The losses come in waves. They seem too much.
The birds desert their perches, the whole flock.
    Art, being art, will last,
But it's hard to believe she can proceed with such
(An old man failing, nodding off to Bach)
    Diminishment of cast.

ON REREADING SOME LINES OF POETRY

How many years have passed since I last read
These quiet lines? It might be five, or more,
Since I last saw them on the silent page
And heard them move across it, like a stream
Deep in the woods, that underneath the sounds
Of birdcall, insect drone, and summer leaves
Jostled by casual turns of a fitful wind,
Keeps up a steady murmur. Once again
I see their even progress in long rows
Broken at intervals by sudden shifts,
As when the contours of a meditation
Are interrupted by the thought of time,
And hear their music, barely music, faint
But sure, so close to the rhythms of the mind
We almost think its movements are our own,
And its contractions and its relaxations
The beating of our hearts.

                        Though it's been years,
The gradual accents of these paragraphs
Have not been music to a deaf man's ear.
For many times, amid the clattering lines
Of other poems, stunned by the fusillade
Of all the notes played every way at once,
Or disappointed by the random jerks
And stumblings of what's merely chopped-up prose
Meandering, or bored past sympathy
By strict, mechanical rigidity,
That stiff, robotic hammering of nails,
How often has my inner ear heard you
As what I wasn't hearing. And, what's more,
How often has the mind, that learned to read
By contemplating your instructive scenes,
Trained by those early lessons, been led on
To elevated moments, when the world
With all its crass distractions falls away,
When all our faculties, in harmony,

Identity Theft

ON REREADING SOME LINES OF POETRY

Combine to focus on a single page,
And, scarcely breathing, silently, with joy,
We see into the life of poems.

                      Or is
This vain delusion? Perhaps. But even so,
O archetype, profound original,
How often have your lines returned to me!

Now, suddenly, my eyes upon your page,
I find myself perplexed. Who was I then,
When I first wandered through your passages
Giddy with revelation? Reading was all
In all, and I believed myself alone
Privy to all your secrets, acolyte
Attendant on secluded meanings veiled
By simple words like "deep" and "quiet" and "joy."
Those days are past. The visionary gleam
No longer flickers in between the lines.
I cannot half-create you, just perceive.
The older man must build his own abode,
As mean as a hermit's hut in the deep woods
If need be, out of what he has at hand,
Not dream the grand baronial chateaux,
"The cloud-capp'd towers, the gorgeous palaces"
That others have erected really his.
But I still hear, though in a minor key,
The muted syllables of sleights of phrase
That conjured worlds within worlds in a flash,
Lighting the secret chambers of their art,
The inner rooms and hidden vestibules
Hung with old tapestries of pastoral scenes
Cast into clear relief. And I still feel
The sublimated sense of something else,
How all our thefts and hopeless jealousies
And petty pleasures, even the cruel words
We turn on others and against ourselves,

ON REREADING SOME LINES OF POETRY

Belie a deeper love, of all we hold
In common trust, those strange, voluminous tomes
In which all art and nature sit inscribed,
Delineated, given their proper terms,
And which inflect all that we think and say
With lush profusion of commingling sense
And prompt, even now, those vivid moments when
The mind and all its reading interfuse
To animate the living, breathing page,
And, the whole world suspended, still inform
These very words, even these very lines.

And were this all inconsequential dream,
Or were I where I could no longer take
These soft but clear impressions, written off
By time itself, marked down, as cold as stone,
It would not matter. For here you are, right now,
My friend, my closest, truest friend, whose eyes
On this page at this moment are all that's left
To me of human sympathy and hope.
I must believe you see these shadowed lines
Lead back to other lines, and understand
The heart that's faithful to its origins
Sits like an open book, for all to read
Who care to, closely, word by chosen word.

Or do the words choose us? These words chose me
And made me who I am. So let the lines
That speak most deeply to your inmost thoughts
Shine on you like the moon, and shape your soul.
Let them blow through you like the mountain winds.
And sometime, when you can, remember me
As one who loved what you love. Remember me.

WHO THEY WERE

1

Long years have passed, but I still grieve,
   In silence, mostly. Poems lie.
   Though we know those we love will die
We don't believe it till they leave

And leave us dropping through thin air
   Like someone who's stepped off a cliff.
   No hypothetical "as if"
Prepares for their not being there.

The ceremonies of farewell
   Force us to put a brave face on,
   To indicate we know they've gone
And gone for good. We might as well

Attend the preacher's formal words
   Of consolation, though they're hollow.
   It's good to have a script to follow
And hymns drowned by the organ's chords.

We mourn for weeks. We grieve for years.
   And long after we've left our cave
   The memory rises like a wave
And swamps us, suddenly in tears.

WHO THEY WERE

2

House where we all grew up, and where
  Both our beloved parents died,
   I see you now, but from outside.
Another family's living there.

Let's hope the parents know how to live
  In rituals of domestic bliss
   And give their children the warm kiss
Only a loving home can give.

We had that, and we had much more,
  Adventures, dinner table games,
   Odd pets with comical nicknames.
I fight the urge to knock on the door

And know I won't be back again.
  It's time to let the past be gone.
   With or without love, life moves on.
I start the car. It starts to rain.

WHO THEY WERE

3

But still those hallways, windows, rooms
    Return in dreams, and give their shape
    To gray material, fringed with crepe.
There's no need for half-acre tombs

When smaller spaces signify
    Much more than we can ever say.
Everyone else has gone away
And left me here, I don't know why,

While faceless forces, out of control,
    Ransack the town. I hide upstairs,
    Abandoning my post. Who cares?
I do, and wake. This takes its toll

Night after night. What's left unsaid
    Finds its way out between our lips
    Through hidden puns and Freudian slips.
Uncanny, words are never dead

And have the power to concentrate
    More meaning than we first conceive.
    Their house is some place I can't leave
Where it's too late and not too late.

WHO THEY WERE

4

But it's too late to leave unsaid
    The wounding words that left their mark,
    Irreverence toward the patriarch,
Or cruel ingratitude. The dead,

We pray, gain some perspective on
    The terms of human frailty
    From where they are. Where that may be,
Who knows? I don't. I know they're gone

But find it comforting to hope
    Not into utter nothingness.
    An unbeliever, more or less,
I know some things beyond my scope.

O Mother, Father, think of me!
    On high in the angelic sphere
    Forgive your poor son, if you hear.
Look on him kindly, if you see.

WHO THEY WERE

5

The lacerations of regret
    Can traumatize our memory.
    Some things we can't change. Let them be.
And though we never quite forget

Sins of omission, selfish acts,
    Failures of character and trust,
    They loved us, and for them we must
Accept ourselves. The heart contracts

In the raw, terminal shock of loss,
    We lurch and stumble, cry and curse
    Whatever, awful, now seems worse,
But something scrubs away the dross

Over the months and years to come,
    Call it their love. The heart expands,
    The surface shines. Through perilous lands
The bewildered spirit wanders home.

WHO THEY WERE

6

Which isn't what it was, a place
    One somehow didn't have to earn,
    With presences to which I'd turn,
My mother's face, my father's face,

But rather a momentary frame
    Of mind, occurring anywhere.
    As golden absences, they're there.
I almost hear them say my name

And patiently start telling me
    Some story I really might have heard
    (The drift is clear, the facts are blurred)
Set back in the vanished century

That amplifies just who they were:
    Old-world yet current, wry, genteel,
    But human, loving, hurtful, real.
I think of him, I think of her

And sense I'm never quite alone,
    With traces of their company
    More present than the world we see,
And then they're gone. I'm on my own.

WHO THEY WERE

7

The season's swallows dip and dive,
    Skimming the surface of the world.
    The clouds command the sky, unfurled
In monstrous blooms. In overdrive

A cold wind sweeps the skittering leaves
    Mounting in corners, clotting gutters.
    Dismayed, the spirit sags and sputters.
Life's rendered now, reduced to greaves

And liquid, not by heat but cold.
    The pale light weakens day by day.
    The summer's warmth seems years away,
A shining, fictive age of gold

Far off as childhood, and less real.
    December, and the day is here.
    Another year. (Another year!)
How much we felt, when we could feel.

WHO THEY WERE

8

And they were children, long ago,
As foreign as that seems to sense.
There's photographic evidence,
Though frail, of scenes that we can't know

Except in sepia-tinted shades
Curled at the edges, yet somehow
Staring right at the here and now.
And something flashes as it fades

Under nostalgia's scrutiny:
For there they are, where we can look
At him, entranced by a picture book,
Or her, pretending to serve tea,

And glimpse the faintest, gentlest trace
Of features we recognize for sure
Crystallized in miniature,
The parent's face in the child's face.

WHO THEY WERE

9

But shut the haunted album there.
   Don't turn from page to freighted page
   To see them changing, stage by stage,
The crinkling face, the thinning hair,

Approaching the last indignities
   In photographic pantomime,
   Succumbing to the dark lord, time,
To withering, crippling illness. Please

Remember them as who they were
   When we were young, and they were strong.
   Though not enough, that lasted long.
Just think of him. And think of her.

WHO THEY WERE

10

High on a hill in Hollywood,
    In Richmond, city of their birth,
        His dust, her ashes return to earth.
The place is peaceful, green. That's good:

What consolation the soul can take
    From well-trimmed lawns and handsome trees
        They take. Or we do. Subtleties
Of cultivation, which we make

In urgencies of present tense
    To say the past was here, and mattered
        (Though suddenly a whole world shattered),
Make meaning where they can't make sense.

What does make sense? The lifelong goals
    Attained when the people who most care
        Are earth and smoke and rain and air?
They were the noblest, bravest souls

It's been my privilege to know.
    I'll leave it there, and recognize
        Their silent, beautiful graves: there lies
Olivia, and there lies Joe.

III. Tropes

SHIP OF TROPE

O build your ship of trope, for you will need it.

When sand from the spreading deserts erodes the monuments,
When cities are abandoned, and tribes have moved to the north,
Your ship of trope will carry what little remains.

When the things our words once named are nothing at all,
You'll need your ship of trope, for what remains.

GUM

after GW

Nyssa or Liquidambar, Eucalyptus,
Or just a gum tree, oozing the viscous, brittle
Non-crystalline guck little by glistening little,
Which, processed, serves for anything that grips us,
Handles, galoshes, bands, belts, multi-ply
Radials, insulation, leotards,
Or sweetening the pack of trading cards
As, crackling, we blast down the road on a sugar high
Until the bubble bursts, the front tires blow,
The belt snaps, and the rookie of the year
Goes bust, big time, to wind up another bum
Just hanging around the bars, an average joe
Chewed up, spit out in the sawdust and spilled beer,
Stuck on the sole of some stranger's shoe,
                                                    like gum.

TOUCH AND GO

Skirting disaster, walking a very fine line
Like the edge of a knife, steering your rickety craft
Between perils (the abstract, the literal) and more
Perils (the pat, the abstruse), then cutting away
From the current to nudge through the shallows (to someone far
Off it may seem you are now merely drifting),
One slip of attention from foundering in oblivion,
Your *Andrew* docked in sand, its dubious cargo
Just flotsam and jetsam, bobbing off or washed up
On the island of Nowhere, never received or recorded,
With no one even to say "And whose was this?,"
An enterprise all risk and little reward,
Each time you pick up a pen it's touch and go,

As in circumstances every bit as dicey
And far more dire, the surgeon with his scalpels,
His clamps and threads, laboring deep in the body,
The bloody instrument precisely firm
As he slices through tissue, opening the heart
In a dark calculus, intervention over
Trauma, as the vital signs wobble and waver
In oscillation one wayward stroke could cut
Blinking into flat-line, all systems gone,
Who, hours later, thoroughly scrubbed and drained,
Must pad down the echoing corridor to speak
With the stunned family suspended in waiting,
And say with mild reassurance and no false hope
He's done the best he can, it's touch and go,

Or the sole climber still far up the mountain, caught out
By a shift in the weather, clouds closing in fast
And the safe way down too long, who inches across
The cliff-face, toe-hold by finger-hold, with the end
Just a flinch away, no belaying rope, no buddy
(What a damned fool to come up here alone, to relish
The heady challenge, then linger, blissed, on the summit,
Drinking in the unwitnessed triumph, the pure,

Identity Theft

TOUCH AND GO

Cold air, the feeling of standing on top of the world),
Who must banish such slippery thoughts, and ignore, at all cost,
The gravity of his predicament,
His muscles cramping, and concentrate on only
The sheer particulars of austere terrain
And taut discipline, finger-grip, toe-grip,
Clutching the rock like his life it's touch and go,

Or Mr. Bixby, as the sun goes down,
Deciding to risk the crossing at Hat Island
To cover his partner's bungle and make the mouth,
The silence broken by the notes of the bell
And the leadsmen, "Labboard lead! Stabboard lead!"
"M-a-r-k three! ... M-a-r-k three! ... Half twain ... Quarter twain ...
  M-a-r-k twain!,"
And as the steam starts whistling through the gauge cocks
He swings the big boat into invisible marks,
She clears the first reef, then the next, and in
Absolute darkness, engines cut, she drifts
With the current, right into the sudden shadow
Cast by the massive head of the island, right on it,
The water shoaler and shoaler, the cries urgent,
"Eight-and-a-half! ... E-i-g-h-t feet! ... Seven-and-a-half ...
Seven feet! ... *Six*" and the ship scrapes bottom
"*Now*, let her have it, every ounce you've got!"
Bells ringing "Put her hard down! Snatch her! Snatch her!"
As the steamer grinds into sand it's touch and go,

And so here goes, the gamble, the desperate shot,
The wing and the flailing prayer, the Hail Mary,
The all-or-nothing go-for-broke buzzer beater
Arcing toward the goal as the light comes on,
Whether the stakes are high life or survival
Or merely the status of the reputation
Even the greenest performer puts on the line
Each time he steps into the spotlit circle
Of everyone's expectations, and his own,

166 | *Identity Theft*

TOUCH AND GO

Knowing the higher you go the farther you fall
With the freedom of anonymity gone forever
And the specter of utter failure always present,
Even for the poet in his rented mansard,
At his hand-me-down writing desk, who blankly stares
Out the window at the world, then down at the page,
Then off in a spectacle of catatonia,
Painted into a corner and paralyzed
As the poem comes right up to a line it can't cross
(Like plagiarizing a great American classic)
And now you have to turn it one last time
As hard as you can—are you ready?—just at the point
The contract threatens to rip under the strain
It's touch and go, *touch* and that would be *go*

PAPER VIEW

It seems, at first, a rudimentary art
With simple tools (just paper, scissors, glue),
Plain objects—maybe mountains, for a start,

Gray triangles against a sky, pale blue—
In basic two-dimensional arrangements
Even a child can work his way into,

Cut, cut, paste, paste, first tentative engagements
With making things like and unlike the world,
That meet the first frustrations and estrangements—

The piece that just fell off, the edge that curled—
And the first giddy rushes of achievement
With which a new, creative self unfurled

In blissful ignorance of pain, bereavement,
Failure, betrayal, alienation, theft,
With no conception of what to conceive meant,

No rivalry with talents much more deft,
No sense that every step you take is weighted
By all the burden that the past has left

To you, "the artist," thoroughly belated
And bounced from school to school right from the start
(Was it too much too soon? should you have waited?

At what point did your task turn into Art?),
Till gradually the darker implications
Insinuate themselves, and every part

Of what you make shows certain indications
Of just how unoriginal you are,
As illustrated by your illustrations

PAPER VIEW

Of archetypal images—the Star,
The Tree, the Wave—all tried but not quite true
To either art or nature (who set the bar?

You jumped, and it came clanking down on you),
And bad enough to trigger your expulsion
From the College of Collage, but though you're through

You're never finished, the disgust, repulsion,
And anger of the audience embitters
But doesn't free you, for your old compulsion

Must quit the carpers as it quits the quitters,
Letting the whole tradition clutter your work—
Picasso, Hamilton, chair caning, Schwitters,

Canned ham, *merz*, ticket stubs, a soda jerk,
Duchamp, cracked glass, a Ballantine beer can,
And, most derivative of the handiwork

Of one not one of a kind, so not the man,
A toy monkey nailed to a screen door
Entitled "Self-portrait as Paul Cézanne"—

Till every piece becomes a metaphor
For meta-art, and you, who never met
A "meta" that you weren't a sucker for,

Sporting allusion like a carcanet,
Become not all but nothing, just a fop
With all the free will of a marionette,

The Man Who Couldn't Start and Couldn't Stop,
Misguided, garbled, a museum tour
At the end of which all sense of art goes POP,

PAPER VIEW

For which the only treatment (there's no cure)
Is back to basics, wiping the dirty slate,
Preparing for a script that's simple, pure

(Though it's late to start over, far too late),
Is to think "craft" not "art," think "not too fast"
Not "now's my chance," think "modest," never "great,"

And never, never think about the Past
Dizzying at its apex—the monument
That is and ends all, being built to last

Until the last to build, the man you meant
To be, adds his great seal, the shining eye
Atop the pyramid, and the ascent

Of art through all the ages touches the sky
And stands complete, NOVUS ORDO SECLORUM,
The quest stops at the caravanserai,

The inn with room for few, the ultimate forum,
Where, handshakes all around, and secret signs,
The pale initiate brotherhood sits in quorum

Feasting on dates and figs and clementines
To welcome one who's been so quintessential—
Cancel such wicked thoughts, erase these lines,

Try something distant, patient, Oriental,
Apprenticing yourself to a vagrant swami
To focus on the spare and elemental,

And, wizardry with scissors, kirigami,
Being ruled out (sharp objects are denied you),
Learn how the crimps and folds of origami

PAPER VIEW

Can summon forth the fiddling child inside you
With shapes like Water Lily, Flapping Bird—
Less tortured than the twisted forms that tried you

And found you wanting, fumbling, thick, absurd—
That, "natural as nature," signify
In the beginning was not, so to speak, the word

And its untrusty sidekick, the bald lie,
But geometric patterns that spring true
As images unfold to train the eye,

Till mimicries with "kami," birch, bamboo,
Take forms that certify or guarantee
(Like the diploma you don't have, folded in two)

A product not unlike the world we see,
Touching the bases—bird, fish, waterbomb—
In the belief a frank simplicity

Can hold the mirror up to dear old Mom
In keeping with mimetic strictures found
Listed at representational.com,

Not understanding you're on shaky ground,
All ground being shaky, Nature being a mess
With no straight edges in a world not round

Where all is fractals, patterned randomness,
And figure, poor figure, something that sticks out
Like someone showing up in evening dress

(Without a clue if not without a doubt)
To a lunchtime barbecue in a trailer park,
Not seeing an elaborate roundabout

PAPER VIEW

Has funneled you back to archetypes, and stark
Knee-jerk reaction's shifting, muddled aims
Have led you to, as always, miss your mark,

And still the mind keeps playing mirror games,
Whether you're riveted or utterly bored
By pinhole perspectives of the view that frames

Receding diagonals of checkerboard
Floors in the paper houses some obscure
Dutch master fashioned out of glue, pasteboard

(You saw them, where and when you can't be sure),
And paint so scientific in detail
Space opens up, and flummoxed by the lure

Of *trompe l'oeil* trickery you're back in jail,
The prison of expectations gone awry,
Seeing Art triumph where you're bound to fail,

The truth is true art lies, and you can't lie
With half the skill to make it all seem true
To even the unsuspecting passerby

At his most gullible, even to you,
And, off your medication, losing your grip,
You tell yourself there's one thing left to do

To terminate this bummer of a trip
And shut up shop, drive home the final nail,
Your *oeuvre*'s crown, a plain gray Möbius strip

That snakes around to swallow its own tail
And, representing nothing, makes an end
Without an end, so yet once more you fail,

PAPER VIEW

Recycling your fool self around the bend
Back to the finish, forward to the start
But knowing, this time, what the signs portend,

Your whole life one long bungled piece of art,
No value in it, just its cost to you,
All the way to the end it breaks your heart

And as you go you pay per paper view

A SPADE A SPADE

It isn't in the cards: that well-worn phrase
That means to speak the truth, to call things straight,
To "tell it like it is" (though there's that "like"),
Without evasion via metaphor,
Isn't to call one's own bluff, naming the suit—
Amid the shufflings of the smoke-filled room,
The sidelong glances, the chips stacked on the baize
Like fortress castles guarding the bends in the Rhine,
The silent faces, the sharpies counting the cards,
The sleights, the false bravura, the dare, the draw—
As anything but diamonds, clubs, or hearts.

The context's farming: naming the implement,
The humble spade, as what it merely is,
And never something as mighty as a shovel.
Its written history goes back to Plutarch,
Quoting Philip on Macedonians
In the *Apophthegmata*, although there
It seems the object to which the phrase refers,
The pure, plain, unalloyed thing itself,
Isn't a spade at all, but rather a trough,
A basin, or a bowl, or even a boat,
Having been mistranslated by Erasmus
And passed, thus garbled, into general use.

It wasn't a spade. Nor was it what we've made it
In parlance English and Americans share,
The sign of honesty, of common sense,
Of virtue, purposed, Puritanical,
Suspicious of language itself, its tricks, its lies,
Its twists of filigree and fol-de-rol
And *double entendres* that seem, well, far too French,
And threaten to sinuously undermine
Those manly qualities we praise and prize
Above all others, founding our civics on
The solid sense our words say what we mean
And nothing else, transparent, under control,

A SPADE A SPADE

Which helps us keep our faces utterly straight,
Our postures rigid, and our upper lips
As stiff as the starched, pressed shirts our leaders wear
As, adults among children, we steer the world.

Far from it. In Plutarch, the Macedonian king
Is telling a visitor his countrymen
Are clownish, rude, uncultured, simple-minded,
In his words, "grosse, clubbyshe, and rusticall,"
Dour, lumpish folk, "they whiche had not the witte
To call a spade by any other name"
(That's Udall, from Erasmus, with the error).
No mark of virtue, then, insistence on
A literal, stark world of denotation
Stripped of all textured resonance, all art,
All turns and colorings of metaphor,
Is rather the sign of a crude stupidity,
Unlettered, mean, suspicious, knuckle-headed,
Incapable of connecting like to like,
Of piecing the world together with the mind,
Of seeing the cream in the surf, the spokes in the dawn.

A spade a spade. A horse a horse. A lark—
You get the picture. (Or, perhaps, you don't.)
But the next time you hear a poet praised
For simple language, and a stripped-down style
Pared clean of all adornment, honest and pure,
For "plain American cats and dogs can read,"
Remember Plutarch's Philip, and ask yourself
If this is really the art that conceals art,
The master's renunciation of his craft,
Its mirror games, its metamorphoses,
Its parabolic sweeps of hyperbole,
Or merely the token of imbecility,
And ask, also, whether the critic who claims
This artless art as art's true apogee
Knows anything at all, beyond the dark

A SPADE A SPADE

Resentments motivating bitter minds
That hate all ornament, all flair, all play,
And, caught at a literal loss by irony,
Lash out in fear the joke might be on them,
Insistent words be unambiguous,
Which isn't in the cards, and furious
That someone else is having a good time.

NAUTICAL TERMS

"Words alone are certain good."

Not all that long ago,
We were nautical folk: barges and sloops,
   Clippers and steamers and sharpies,
Were how we got wherever we had to go,
     Moved goods and troops
     Or fled Virgilian harpies,
As if all destinations were the slips
     Where we could dock our ships.

   That's changed, of course: sports car
And jumbo jet, r. v. and high-speed train,
     Aiming at stations, lots,
And carpeted ports, carry us near and far
      Through wind and rain
     To plush vacation spots
That proffer heated pools and personal trainers.
     Now ships are for containers.

   But as we moved on we
Carried the signs of our sea-faring phases
     Embedded in language itself.
We glide like shadows miles above the sea,
      But common phrases
     Accrete like an ocean shelf,
Layer on layer, sedimental, slow,
     To tell more than we know.

   For did we *know the ropes*,
We'd hear the echoes of maritime concerns
     Haunting the current cline,
Like sextants, compasses, and telescopes
      Guiding our turns
     Of phrase: we *toe the line*,
End up *over the barrel*, or get *dressed down*
     Lest we screw up and drown.

NAUTICAL TERMS

Old senses linger, whether
We're stuck *in the doldrums* like a floating jail
    Or *buoyed up*. We say,
Without much thought, that we're *under the weather*.
    Dark skies prevail,
    Then there's *the devil to pay*:
Like waves, old moods well up and *overwhelm*
    The logic *at the helm*.

    Then, to escape our funk,
We *tie one on*, and, *three sheets to the wind*,
    We wind up *in the head*
Or *over the rail, groggy*, falling-down drunk.
    We're caught, we're ginned
    (We'd be better off dead)
Between the devil and the deep blue sea,
    Footloose, not fancy free.

    Since cautionary tales
Abound, like perils, on the salty freeway,
    The sea's our strategic crib.
No great shakes? Take the wind out of his sails.
    He warrants *leeway*?
    Noting *the cut of his jib*
We *give a wide berth* to the *son of a gun*,
    With room to *cut and run*.

    Though context, *by and large*,
Has *gone by the board*, language doesn't *start*
    Over with a clean slate.
Words get *pressed into service*, with a charge
    That's worlds apart.
    At *the bitter end* it's late,
We've garbled it all, not knowing, our *logbooks* shut,
    The linguistic *scuttlebutt*.

NAUTICAL TERMS

    How many years before
Our most precise locutions, our most fine
      Inflections and gradations
Of subtle sense, mean nothing anymore,
         Dead on the line?
      What unforeseen mutations
Will wrench our phrases, context overthrown,
      Particulars unknown?

    A cautionary tale:
Like Corinth, Babylon, and Jericho
      Splintered to shards and scraps,
So too such terms. They're terminal. Detail
        Will blur and go.
      Philologists, perhaps,
Will piece together something of the past
      We were, who did not last.

    Way back when we were young
We clambered up the rigging. At full sail,
      We flew. Who could misread,
Or "the mysmetre for defaute of tonge"?
        How could words fail?
      They're all we have, indeed.
We had not sung so surely had we known
      They'd soon be on their own.

IV Odes

IV Odes

TO AN ALDABRAN TORTOISE, DEAD AT 250

    The races of the swift,
      Who swiftly come and go
Like fads or pop stars, trending out of sight
Almost before we see them, given their gift
      For getting something right
      For fifteen minutes or so,
The one-hit wonders, overnight sensations,
      Pet Rocks and Salad Shooters,
Or former latest software innovations
      For Pleistocene computers,

    Seem briefer next to you,
      Known as "the only one,"
Adwaitya, oldest sentient thing alive
By eighty years or more, a tortoise who
      Was once the pet of Clive
      Of India. That sun
Set eons since, through veils of saffron dye
      And wafture of a fan,
And while you cast a cold chelonian eye
      On many a vanished man.

    (Not least that lapsed grandee,
      The prototypical
Nabob and potentate, big gun for hire
To profit the East India Company,
      That junkie, thief, and liar
      Who "owned" you, whose steep fall,
Spectacularly public, stunned the nation,
      Who did confess, when tried,
Astonishment at his own moderation,
      Ending a suicide.)

    Now you, whose lifespan spanned
      Mozart and Bird and Cage,
Wordsworth and Motherwell, Turner and Kees,
Plus Kean and Keaton, Kierkegaard and Rand,

TO AN ALDABRAN TORTOISE, DEAD AT 250

    Forests of old-growth trees,
    The whole Industrial Age,
Isms galore, old worlds and new world orders,
    Epochs and epistemes,
Innumerable maps redrawing borders
    For botched colonial schemes,

    Antediluvian,
    Lugging your great domed shell
For centuries, have crossed the finish line
Alone, one of a kind. Small things began
    Your terminal decline:
    For months you'd not been well;
A crack in your armor festered, gnawed by rats;
    Your liver failed; you, too,
Succumbed to time, with no more caveats,
    Dead at the Alipore Zoo.

    Still your trajectory,
    From coralline atoll
To editorial encomia
Upon your death, implies a larger story,
    Of how you came to be a
    Star of sorts, in the role
Of figure for time itself, through silent, sheer
    Endurance of life's stages
On a vast, sidereal scale, year after year
    Bridging the distant ages.

    We fight, we cry, we laugh:
    You turn your head and blink
And we are gone. Or were. For now you are
No longer our living, breathing chronograph,
    Or Vishnu's avatar
    (The second one, I think),
"Kurma," the tortoise, sent to earth to plumb
    The bottom of the ocean

TO AN ALDABRAN TORTOISE, DEAD AT 250

For what we've lost. The cold depths. Chthonic. Dumb.
A whole world in slow motion.

TO AMARYLLIS

Cold Amaryllis, don't think I've forgotten,
After so many years and so many loves,
The cunning words, let fly with barely a shrug,
    That slit my chest wide

Open, slicing my self-esteem to little
Pieces. It's funny, the things we remember
So precisely, and how the kindnesses of
    Other women, more

Recent, more sincere, settle in silence, while
Your casual cruelties, tossed off in a
Moment some twenty years ago, still echo
    As if just spoken.

Your skilled intonations of calculated
Indifference—yes, our affair was over,
And, well, no, you hadn't told me, it wasn't
    Important enough

To bother—were masterful, I'll admit, and,
Like the work of a true artist, made to last.
I have to admire the transferential ease
    With which you transformed

Your resentment of the other to my self-
Hatred. That put an end to things, once and for
All, as you intended, except for this, a
    Belated complaint

Which doubtless will never reach you to hurt you
Who are aging now, childless and embittered,
And have forgotten we were ever in love
    If we ever were.

TO THE REPUBLIC

What have we done, who once were hailed
Protectors of humanity
And celebrated where we sailed,
Whose freedom set the ages free
To scheme what better states could be?
We're symbols of a deadlier sort,
Bullies despised for cruelty,
And I remain despairing of the port.

We should have known what war entailed.
Our fool imperial fantasy
Tried to command the world, and failed.
The consequences we now see:
Explosions of pure misery,
With half a million lives cut short
By death throes of democracy,
And I remain despairing of the port.

Where were the leaders who should have railed
Against such blatant idiocy
Before we launched this shit? They bailed.
Torture and illegality
Have turned our country's policy.
To import oil, we must export
American hypocrisy,
And I remain despairing of the port.

The winds grow violent. History
Breaks empires on the rocks, for sport.
Our sails are rent, we're lost, at sea,
And I remain despairing of the port.

TO GEORGE WASHINGTON IN BALTIMORE

"Great Washington, too, stands high aloft on his towering main-mast in Baltimore, and like one of Hercules' pillars, his column marks that point of human grandeur beyond which few mortals will go ... But neither great Washington, nor Napoleon, nor Nelson, will answer a single hail from below, however madly invoked to befriend by their counsels the distracted decks on which they gaze; however it may be surmised, that their spirits penetrate through the thick haze of the future, and descry what shoals and what rocks must be shunned." — *Moby Dick*, xxxv

        When Ishmael, perched high
On the swaying mast-head, scanned the panoptic view
Under an uneventful tropical sky
        Like a crow atop a tree,
        His drowsy weather eye
"Lost in the infinite series of the sea,"
The languid repetition, blue on blue
        As far as he could see,
        He thought of Nelson, you,

        Napoleon, two set
In stone, one cast in bronze, polished and posted
On towering columns for centuries, to let
        A monumental pose,
        Stiff as an epithet
("Great Washington"), cold gravitas, impose
The elevated qualities thus boasted
        In laudatory shows,
        Feted, hurrahed, and toasted,

        On future generations
(Imperial ambition, martial skill,
Brave sacrifice, the fatherhood of nations,
        Etcetera), to raise
        Our civic aspirations
With trophies that instill a thirst for praise,
Commemorations of the rock-hard will
        To triumph. Those were the days.
        And now? You stand there, still.

        Napoleon can see,
Beyond the hôtels of the Place Vendôme

TO GEORGE WASHINGTON IN BALTIMORE

The Place de la Concorde, the Tuilleries,
　　The Louvre, Musée d'Orsay,
　　　　Perhaps l'Orangerie,
The buttresses of St. Germain de Prés,
A panoply of pantile, spire, and dome
　　On classical display,
　　　　While Nelson is at home

　　　　Watching the circus of
Buses and tourists flocking Trafalgar Square
(Like pigeons the locals hate, the yokels love),
　　　　Surveying Whitehall to
　　　　Big Ben looming above
Parliament and Westminster (Waterloo
Is probably occluded, even from there),
　　　　A famous scene, but you
　　　　Assume a lofty air

　　　　To witness Baltimore
(*Some* national icons have all the luck)
Descend from pleasant city to dirt poor
　　　　Urban calamity,
　　　　And wonder ("never more")
What happened to the world you rose to see,
Displaced by the one with which you're likely stuck
　　　　For what eternity
　　　　Is left before you (*fuck*):

　　　　The Bromo Seltzer Tower
Minus the plastic bottle, City Hall
Unmarred by the foul smokestacks of the Power
　　　　Plant, and these are the high-
　　　　Lights, duller every hour,
As Federal Hill, the water, by and by
Were screened from view by architectural
　　　　Embarrassment, the sky-
　　　　Scrapers' obtrusive wall,

Identity Theft | 189

TO GEORGE WASHINGTON IN BALTIMORE

Along, at least, with "Harble
Place," as the uninspired generic twin
Harbor pavilions are mocked in the Balmer garble
    Of English at its worst.
    Forget yourself to marble?
Would that you could. It wasn't this bad at first,
Or back in the Age of Gold (well, Hammered Tin),
    Before the bubble burst
    And the rowhouse roofs caved in.

    A century ago,
When Henry James, all sensibility,
Absorbed the American scene, he came to know
    Astonishingly soon,
    In half an hour or so
Beneath your simple pomp ("pleasant jejune"),
"A kind of mollified vivacity"
    That richly silent June,
    "A perfect felicity"

    That charmed him, street by street,
This "cheerful little city of the dead"
(But "was it cheerful," or "resigned and discreet"?),
    The "door-stepped houses" rows
    Of "elegant" and "neat"
"Quiet old ladies, seated with their toes
Tucked-up on uniform footstools," prim, well-bred,
    And found such trim tableaus
    Endearing, or so he said,

    Though also, wordily wise,
He paused to register a "still small shock"
At finding "the bourgeois," and to "recognize"
    The Muse of History,
    And in her "strange deep eyes"
The shadow of the War for slavery.
You were like a "stately old-fashioned clock"
    Guarding a parlour he
    Examined to unlock

TO GEORGE WASHINGTON IN BALTIMORE

    Family secrets told
By the tone of things (furniture, *objets d'art*,
Domestic treasures bought with what we sold
        Our land for, "treasures of Style"),
        And from such manifold
Odd decorative pieces of domicile
Information, he measured who we are,
        Noticing, all the while,
        The perspectival jar

    Peculiar to our nation,
Where vulgar intervals (like brownstone) cast
A lingering illusion of duration
        On antecedent stages,
        A temporal "consecration":
Decades turn centuries; centuries, ages;
The fairly recent "nobly antique." The past
        Assembling in his pages
        Was subtle. That didn't last.

    If our observant guest
Were here today, he'd get a larger shock
(Not that anywhere else would pass his test).
        Though ironies are rich,
        We're poor in what we're best
At: gaffes of formstone; tacky sins of kitsch
Like "window art"; TV rooms crammed with schlock;
        The street smack ("Fuck you bitch!");
        The crack houses; the Block.

    Aesthetics? Don't be absurd.
We live in a time and place where anything goes.
Would the Master entertain the Spoken Word?
        Or groove on 98
        Rock? High-five the Bird?
Exquisitely expert, concatenate
The history of taste with *Pink Flamingoes*?
        Deign to participate
        In workshops? Pick up lingoes?

TO GEORGE WASHINGTON IN BALTIMORE

He would, above it all,
See you still there, observing all along
With lidless eyes, cool, imperturbable,
    Constantly unsuspended,
    But not uncomical:
If glanced at from a certain unintended
Perspective, something's hilariously wrong,
    As your right arm, extended,
    Seems an enormous dong

    (Made longer by your right
Hand's grip on a sheaf of paper—more of that),
"The father of our country pose," a sight
    The Master did not see
    Or did not mention. Quite
Embarrassing, even for you, to be
So flagrantly exposed to seamy, scat-
    Ologic ribaldry,
    Though you, of course, don't bat

    An eye, being inured
To the slings and arrows public figures come
To count on from the public, which can't be cured
    Of bouts of ritual
    Abuse, and resting assured
Your rigid pose, stiffly mechanical
(That arm, held out forever, must be numb),
    Is vastly preferable
    To something really dumb:

    The original design
Envisioned you decked out in Roman dress,
Steering a horse-drawn chariot, in line
    With conventional depictions
    Of Power, palatine,
Timelessly sovereign, shaped by the fictions
We fashion to memorially impress,
    Oblivious of restrictions
    Like the financial distress

TO GEORGE WASHINGTON IN BALTIMORE

Of rampant overrun
That led the overseers to scrap that plan –
A scaled-down tribute being better than none
    Given shrinking resources—
    And choose what could be done
Sans balconies, sans chariot, sans horses,
And closer to the essence of the man.
    (Reality enforces.
    We do the best we can.)

    Thus you stand dressed as normal
(Overcoat, trousers, wig), holding that sheaf
In a gesture somehow casual yet formal
    (That half-detached position,
    Nuanced, seemed to inform all
"Great Washington" did), finished with your mission
To free the states for good, in plain relief
    Resigning your commission
    As first Commander in Chief,

    Just like the man himself
(As if he saw what might be from your tower,
Sensing the rocks, the shoals, the hidden shelf,
    The slaughtering of factions
    Like Ghibelline and Guelph,
The bloody, Thermidorian reactions
Of vicious states) took, in his finest hour,
    That most rare of actions
    And gave up all his power.

    Let Napoleon have
Paris (where he's been up and down, to say
The least, considered a hero or a knave
    As each republic lists
    In accents sometimes grave,
Sometimes acute, given to leftist twists
Or rightist turns depending who holds sway,
    Toppled by royalists
    And by Gustave Courbet,

TO GEORGE WASHINGTON IN BALTIMORE

Who fled to beat the rap,
A crippling fine), and let Lord Nelson keep
London beneath his gaze, athwart his cap-
    Stan in an action shot
    And caked in pigeon crap
Spoiling his Creigleith sandstone: you'll take your lot
And stay in Baltimore (write it and weep)
    To stand for what they're not
    On heights where the fall is steep.

(And let that holy fool,
Saint Simeon Stylites, keep his post
As pioneer of the ascetic school
    And connoisseur of pain,
    His body but a tool
That frost, heat, hail, damp, sleet, and wind, and rain
Compete, year in, year out, to punish most
    For spiritual gain,
    And gory is the host

    With maggots to his aid,
Hair shirts, spiked collars, flagellation, burns,
The bitter instruments of the martyr's trade,
    Whose use, however sick,
    Is how the game is played
By arts that study the next difficult trick,
Like sacrificing imagery for urns
    Of polished rhetoric
    Taking its costly turns.)

    No tyrant and no martyr,
Not covetous of an imperial crown,
Stigmata, nor the Order of the Garter,
    Steady in your good name
    You wouldn't smirch or barter
For anything, unmoved by your own fame,
I wonder what you think as you look down
    (With pride? or growing shame?)
    To your eponymous town

TO GEORGE WASHINGTON IN BALTIMORE

      And its huge monument
Sleek as a rocket, one brute phallic thrust
Piercing the heavens with muscular intent,
      Its monstrous obelisk
      A pointed message sent
Without diplomacy, streamlined and brisk,
To all the little nations: "In guns we trust";
      "We call the game, it's Risk";
      "Submit"; "Empire or bust."

      "Great Washington" knew war,
Knew power, knew honor, was not for sale.
You're just a statue, true, but standing for
      A slippery ideal
      Of statecraft, civil, more
Enlightened, subject to the commonweal,
And monolithic simulacra fail,
      Grotesque, malign, unreal
      Beside your human scale.

TO MY FRIENDS

My good friends, when you're under the illusion
That the common end of things has ended me,
Whether that end was sudden or wretchedly slow,
Peaceful or violent, untimely or, finally, wished for,

Don't spend too much time grieving, as if I were gone
To some murky underground region of swampy water
And cavernous absence, metallic and silent and cold,
Or some plush resort in the stratosphere of our dreams

Pillowed with cumuli, graced by ethereal muzak,
Or some massive confusing impersonal processing center
With lines and obscure snafus and numbers not names,
Away from the sun and the sound of the wind in the trees,

But after a short ceremony, public or private,
Listen for the wings of the birds, and ask where we're going,
Alabama or Delaware, Canada, Yucatán,
And wish me luck in the next life, who now have wings.

SHAKESPEARE'S HORSE

We now stood in the Hidden Library of the Palacio Barolo. A familiar but not quite recognizable music was faintly audible. The rooms were all sizes, furnished in various styles, and their arrangement was odd: single rooms, sometimes quite large, led to suites of three connected rooms, which led in turn to another single room. When I asked the purpose of this design, my guide smiled. "I wish I could remember whether I thought to put that question to Palanti while he was still alive," he replied. "But if I did, I don't recall his answer, if he answered at all. And even had he answered, I doubt he would have told me the truth, if he knew the truth."

—J. H. Hobson, *Six Days in Buenos Aires*

TO C

Let Dominica be the essence of green,
The florabundance of banana farms
With Sisserou and Jaco raiding the fruit,
Green birds, green fruit, green trees with massive leaves
Nodding in hillside waves at every breeze
That rolls in off the wild Sargasso sea
Accumulating mountainous evidence
Of afternoon's appointment with the rain,

And let the ochre dust of Roussillon
Signify the range of orange and red,
The rose and russet houses and placettes,
Sun-burned, eroded bluffs, and the dry air
Enveloping the hill-top sanctuaries
That overlook the windswept Luberon,
The painterly gradations that define
Light in the lavender summers of Provence,

And let the cobbled streets of Orvieto
Exemplify the purples and deep reds
Half visible beneath the gray patine
Now settled on blocchetti de porfido
Ascending toward the striped kaleidoscope,
The shimmering mosaic of facade
On the great Duomo, eclectic miracle
Perched on a tufa cliff in Umbria ...

In other lives we might have lived elsewhere,
Stunned by the carmine skyscapes of the west,
Or bundled tight against the polar cold
In crisp, astringent, boreal purity,
Or meditating in a bamboo hut
As sunrise floods the fields of Celebes,
Or listening to insects half the night
In fragrant torpor, drowsy and tropical,

TO C

But here we are, in the middle of our lives,
In Baltimore, of all places, and satisfied
With modest comforts and a decent house,
Good friends, good food, and leisure to do as we please,
Even to travel for color, but coming home
To make our lives up in the airy dwelling
On into evening lightening with laughter
Where being here together is enough.

WINDSOCK

This conical textile tube to show
    Wind direction and speed
        At sites with a need
            To know

(Airports, bridges, chemical plants)
    Senses, coming or going,
        Just what's blowing
           On, slants

To orient at about three
    Knots, extends at fifteen,
        Flutters between,
           Limps free

As it dies down, taking the measure
    Of elemental force,
        Or serves, of course,
           Our pleasure

In bright things that ripple and float
    For decorative show
        On patio
           Or boat,

Proving, if manufactured well,
    Something quite frail and slight,
        Set at a height,
           Can tell

Something essential about our world
    And, being empty, can fill
        Or fall, be still
           Or swirled

WINDSOCK

In keeping with what's current, here
And now (what, powerful,
May whip, or lull,
Or shear),

Can, flapping, indicate, if placed
Domestically—just check
The gimcrack deck—
Our taste

In style and color (Santa, Seal,
Pirate, Tropical Fish,
Whatever you wish,
Puce, teal),

But, *pace* ancestors in the Far
East, where on high display
Each Children's Day
They star

As signs of luck, longevity
And sons, streamlined and sharp
Black and red carp
At sea

In rushing air (some houses have none,
Bitter end of the line),
Cannot decline
The pun

That finally whistles into place
When blindingly, at last,
The wind will blast
Your face.

TO PLUTO, UPON ITS DECLASSIFICATION

The word is out you're out, the ninth of nine
—Perhaps we wanted nine, like lives, or muses—
No longer. Fundamentals realign.
You've been unchosen as the new rule chooses,

"Declassified" by analytic tools
That say you're not the real thing, shown the door
Like doping medalists or discredited schools
Stripped of status for having rigged the score,

Dropped from the rolls, kicked off the podium,
Banished to outer rings of history
To orbit in perpetual odium
Or frigid wastes of pure obscurity,

Except you never committed any wrong.
You are the frozen sphere you always were
Before discovery, hurtling along
(Even in telescopes you're just a blur)

Your odd, elliptical trajectory,
"Highly eccentric," the same brown icy ball
Out in the Kuiper Belt's zone of debris,
Luminous for your size, but very small

By planetary standards, which apply
No longer. We'll redesign the orreries,
The planetaria. The naked eye
Won't miss you among all it never sees.

But will you miss the dazzling company,
Lavish, ambrosial, on Olympian heights,
Of Neptune, Jupiter, and Mercury,
Downgraded to hang out with lesser lights

TO PLUTO, UPON ITS DECLASSIFICATION

Like Xena, Orcus, Makemake, Eris,
And Charon, your faithful, binary system moon?
How can a cosmic bum's rush not embarrass?
Who else will get reclassified? How soon?

And do we think such sleights of category
Will free us from dark thoughts of the underworld,
Of subterranean levorotatory
Landscapes where the murky waters, swirled

By deep rip tides, emit a noxious mist,
Where Sisyphus keeps slipping in the muck,
And scattered like brittle leaves, like windswept grist,
The darkling souls lament, eternally stuck

On the wrong side of Acheron or Styx?
The arguments are over, the die is cast
Like votes at a convention, and the fix
Approved, and in. You're out, no longer last,

And join the lengthening list of the demoted,
The cast off, airbrushed out, and sent back down,
The deanthologized, no longer noted
Inhabitants of Nowhere, a ghost town:

Ben Johnson, Harold Stassen, the Aral Sea,
Pomerania, Steam, Hanno the Great,
The mineral kingdom of taxonomy
And too many poets to enumerate,

Like Abraham Cowley, famous for being forgotten,
Once thought the peer of Milton, who admired him,
Whose "learned puerilities" and misbegotten
Pindaric cucumbers to what inspired him

TO PLUTO, UPON ITS DECLASSIFICATION

Displayed his "lax and lawless versification,"
His negligence of diction, all the flaws
Exposed in Johnson's firm consideration,
Which exiled and preserved him. The harsh laws

Art yields to over time, massive attrition,
Survival of the fewest, raze and burn,
Position most of us in worse position.
Period pieces crack. The worm does turn,

While he still circles somewhere, scarcely read,
Tracing his faint ellipsis in the stark,
Chill nether regions of the all but dead,
Abysmal vacuums of Plutonian dark.

AFGHAN KITES

Although
At a first glance
A visitor might think
Them birds, or bits of colored paper
Spun by the wind in a tropospheric dance
As far overhead they lift and sink,
Curvet, dip, and caper
As if by chance,
This show

Is not
Just prettiness
In curlicues of flight,
Harmonic, terpsichorean,
But quick maneuvering under the stress
Of an all-out aerial fight
Combatants glory in,
Asking finesse,
A lot

Of string,
And racing will
To dive and wheel full speed,
Braving the endless, perfect blue
At altitudes of agonistic skill
Where puffed-up boast succumbs to deed
And weakness is cut through
To pain or thrill
(They sing

AFGHAN KITES

        Of that
      Day still). And these
    Frail artifacts of bright,
  Thin paper and whittled bamboo,
Far from mere brilliant toys crafted to please
  When unspooled to a dazzling height,
    Are framed and fashioned to,
      With wicked ease,
        Combat

        Both air
      And other kites,
    Across whose wires they slice
  Their own *tars* caked in an armored coat
Composing the edges of these scintillant fights
  (Adhesive, ground glass, and mushed rice)
    So, severed, off they float
      In pointless flights
        To where

        The street
      Boys run them down,
    Finders keepers, or "free
  And legal." The game plays when it can,
Catastrophe permitting, all over town,
  Defying mullahs who can't see
    ("Ban, ban, Taliban")
      Beyond their own
        Conceit.

AFGHAN KITES

Intact,
The sharp truth smarts:
Beauty is ruthless, and
It needs to be, given the at-
Mospherics and the odds, the moving parts
(Whipping *tars* will ribbon a hand
Or slit a throat, like that).
Way off the charts
The act

Is still
Appointed for
Wind-hammered heights of play
Both festival and hazardous,
As beauty and valor, air, pride, plume, and more
Buckle in turn and are blown away,
Whatever they meant to us
Who knew the score,
The kill.

WAKEFIELD

Start with the moral: the fabric of our lives,
Their texture of connection, from leitmotif
To puniest detail, the slipshod rooms,
The mismatched furniture, the slapdash walls,
Down to the knickknacks and the silly clock,
Is interwoven so precariously
One blunder, one fool act, one stupid word
Blurted in half-distracted thoughtlessness
Could be the casual tug on the causal thread
That starts the intricate tapestry of affection,
Allegiance, habit, comfort, and resolve
Unraveling. It dangles, beckoning
Some imp within us, curst, contrarian,
Some brat defying the parental "no"
To touch the hot plate, open the car door,
Let go the guiding hand and dart away
Into the perilous, concealing crowd,
Discovering the self in self-destruction.

Or uncovering its absence, for in fact
This is our queasiest, most nervous fear:
Our cultivated sense of who we are
Depends on simple ignorance of the weird,
Unruly laws that fashion identity
Through destinies as flippant as caprice.
We went to X not Y, we took the job
In Starkville, in an inexplicable funk
We broke it off, we opted to buy in
Two months before the firm went belly up.
These aren't the best examples; they contain
Traces of impulse or velleity.
The accident at the crosswalk, the canceled flight,
The arsonist who moved in up the street,
These are our secret factors, the instruments
That seize our ends, rough-hew them how they will,
And strand us, outcasts of the universe.

WAKEFIELD

Thus Wakefield, a man to all appearances
Vaguely unremarkable, middle-aged,
A little heavyset, of average height,
And though respectable not at all distinguished,
Afflicted by a certain sluggishness
One might mistake for mere complacency,
If intellectual just lazily so,
A bit too fond of some intoxicant,
And to those who knew him best, mainly his wife,
Displaying a trivial pleasure in deception
Giving the slightest hint what was to come:
One evening he left home on a short trip,
Purpose unspecified, and didn't return
For more than twenty years, when, out of the blue
(To be more accurate, out of the rain)
He simply showed back up, resumed his place,
And remained a regular husband until his death.

The reason for this hiatus? There wasn't one.
No mistress whose passion made his wife seem stale,
Whose amorous titillations led him off
Into a roller coaster pas de deux
Until she threw him out, or left, or died,
Or the thrill of the illicit wore away
Till what remained was tawdry, awkward, fraught
With recrimination and a dull regret
That made him long for everything he'd spurned,
His fireside, books, and rocker, and a wife
Whose placid toleration calmed his nerves.
No secret crime he vanished to conceal
Or spend the fruits of, till the long entr'acte
Elapsed without discovery, or the few
Cognizant of his fraud had passed away,
Persuading him the coast was finally clear.
No accident that left the man confused
And injured, isolated in a town
Where no one knew who he was or especially cared,

WAKEFIELD

Until, years later, some erratic spark,
A smell, a voice, the mention of a place
Ignited a synapse, and point by point his world
Swam back into focus, like a metropolis
Minute by minute emerging from a fog,
The street lamps, sidewalks, doorways, finials
Gradually clarifying, and, still dazed,
Half-blind in sudden sunlight, he knew his way
Back to his distant harbor, if not his name.

As it turned out, he hadn't even left town,
Just rented a flat in an adjacent street,
Planning, at first, only the briefest stay,
A break from habitude, to clear his mind,
And also, maybe, to unnerve his wife,
So self-assured in her sedate routine.
But this odd, momentary interruption
Gathered a drift and purpose of its own,
Seemed to acquire its own strange lassitude,
Its own inertia settling in for good.
So days turned into weeks, weeks into years.
He grew a beard and whiskers, altered his dress,
Adopting a shabbier, bohemian style,
Spoke with a trace of accent, found new haunts,
Took different work under a different name
And reveled in the dark, elaborate joke
Of having vanished under everyone's nose,
Till even his pleasure in that seemed nothing more
Than fantasies of someone else's life.

To pull this off at close proximity
Was possible only in a teeming hive
Like London, swarming with humanity
And the intimate anonymity of crowds.
Everyone looks like someone, or so they say.
He didn't even avoid his former house,
But almost daily would slink past the spot,

WAKEFIELD

Though always on the other side of the street,
Protected from detection by carriages,
Pedestrians, and a row of sickly trees.
He watched his wife, first shaken, then in black,
Plod on about her errands as in a dream,
Witnessed her slow recovery, her descent
Into a dull, autumnal loneliness.
And sometimes, in the evening, he beheld
Her shadow cast by firelight, her nose and chin
Distorted in dancing, flickering grotesque,
Like some old witch of folklore, up from the depths.
But eventually these skulking visitations
Grew more infrequent, then stopped, having come to seem
A pointless repetition, a return
To something no longer even a little strange.

One evening, quite by accident, he found
Himself outside the old place, lost in thought.
It had been one of those dour London days
When steel-gray storm clouds blanket a sunless sky,
Listless and motionless, holding the threat
Of a thorough soaking over everyone's head
With occasional passing splatters, but holding off
Till it darkens a little too quickly as the wind
Picks up the jettisoned papers, the trees sway,
The awnings flap, the atmosphere heaves and shudders
And a drumroll announces the collisional boom
As all hell breaks loose, pounding the cobblestones
At narrowing angles, streaming the windowpanes
And flooding the gutters, the world is aslant and awash
And drenched to the shivering bone, and Wakefield, jolted
Into the present moment, recognizes
The firelight caressing the parlor window, and sees,
In a flash, himself as that ludicrous thing, a man
Lacking the sense to come in out of the rain,
And in a surge of whimsy ascends the stairs,
Raps the familiar knocker, and enters his home.

WAKEFIELD

Or so Nathaniel Hawthorne figured it,
Pondering the story in his little room
Under the eaves, the "dismal and squalid chamber"
Where he labored in painful anonymity.
Fanshawe a failure he was so ashamed of
He'd thrown his only copy on the fire,
How could he stand it? What was he waiting for?
His mother and sisters, quietly, downstairs,
Took most of their meals apart, not to disturb
The fledgling artist's curious agony.
Would it be possible simply to walk away,
To disappear in Boston, or New York,
Or even, perhaps, in London, and disavow
A life that had narrowed to too blunt a point?
Promise, ambition, expectation, trust:
These are the stuff of nightmare, not of dreams.
Imagining Wakefield he could almost conceive
The man he might become if he let go
And let himself go under, slipping down
The decomposing shifts of solitude.

I understand, I think. For several months
I've been in London on sabbatical,
In a small, walk-up flat in Belsize Park,
Working, in theory, on another book.
I've got my Pakistani takeaway,
My well-worn pub, my corner for cake and tea.
Hardly a thing gets written, but no one minds.
I don't think about my colleagues, who strike me
As absurdly self-important, painfully dull
In all the ways some academics are,
Absorbed in the utter trivialities
Of vicious internecine plots and coups.
And if for a while I thought about my wife
That's lessening, and I am fine without
Her cavalcade of fresh anxieties,
Imagined faux pas, timorous protocols,

WAKEFIELD

And need to redecorate something every week.
There I exaggerate, but not by much.
I love my wife, or did, perhaps do still,
Just not as much as I love having nothing to do
But sit and read without taking a single note,
And forget what I was thinking, or what I am:
A minor talent who didn't live up to that.

But that's all past. Arrangements have been made
To transfer funds to an off-shore account.
It isn't a fortune, but it will be enough.
I've taken another flat, I won't say where.
When my flight leaves tomorrow I won't be on it.
My colleagues will feel self-righteously justified,
Having long thought me "unprofessional,"
A label I've always embraced, to their chagrin.
My wife will be bewildered and, yes, hurt,
Or her pride will be, but she will quickly find,
Being attractive, wealthy, and a flirt,
A man who is better suited for soirees
And fundraisers, and will take a livelier interest
In the politics of arranging dinner parties.
No one will miss me much, I'm relieved to say,
And I won't miss me either, as I was.
I think I'll read all of Trollope, then do it again.
I've finished the final meal I'll put on this card:
Bone marrow and parsley salad, which was superb,
Followed by saddle of rabbit with butterbeans,
Accompanied by Châteauneuf-du-Pape
And rounded off with a sip of Courvoisier.
All that remains is to settle up the bill,
Return to my rental, pack, and finish this,
The very last poem you'll ever have from me.

TO QUINTUS MINIMUS

Catullus cxvii

May all the vulnerable young
Steer clear of you, Quintus, you scoundrel
Hounding the helpless, you brow-beating
Pedant, sticking your stupid
Opinions all over their poems.

TO GALLIENUS

"He was a master of several curious but useless sciences, a ready orator, and elegant poet, a skilful gardener, an excellent cook, and a most contemptible prince."—Gibbon

Gallienus, buried under centuries
Of opprobrium for your pompous inattention
    As the empire veered into chaos,
    Shrugging off invasions
    And plagues with a quotable quip,
Roused, when roused at all, to punitive cruelties,
Slaughtering young and old throughout Illyricum,

You total disaster (though a talented fellow,
Master of sciences curious but useless,
    Well-spoken and good in the kitchen,
    Reciting elegant poetry
    At ridiculous banquets, and doing
Whomever wherever, who blew off a crisis
Considering esoterica with Plotinus),

What, really, could *you* have done, with thirty tyrants,
Franks in Galicia, Goths in Ephesus,
    The Suevi with their hair-knots
    Crossing the Alps, and your father,
    Worthy Valerian,
Skinned and stuffed with straw and hauled about
In hideous effigy? Repress it all.

Who needs the linen of Egypt, the arras of Gaul?

TO AENEAS SILVIUS ON MONTE AMIATA

"In the cool air of the hills, among the old oaks and chestnuts, on the green meadow where there were no thorns to wound the feet, and no snakes or insects to hurt or annoy, the Pope passed days of unclouded happiness."—Burkhardt

Ambitious worldling, ubiquitous diplomat,
Adept at shifting sides a little faster
Than turns of Fortune's wheel, perfecting that
Leap from the falling to the rising master,
Imperial laureate, reluctant pastor,
Backroom maneuverer with sufficient skill
To supersede Guillaume d'Estouteville,

For whom taking orders was relinquishing
Venus for Bacchus, who matured to be
"The man who had a heart for everything,"
From nature, doctrine, art, cosmography,
And ruined riddles of antiquity
To boat races and feasts, shrewd city planner,
Suasive orator in the classic manner,

You sired two bastards, true, when young, and wrote
A smutty literary curio,
But on deliverance from a storm-tossed boat
Piously, though the path was frozen slow,
Walked ten miles barefoot through the ice and snow
To pray at the nearest shrine, as you had vowed,
And suffered pain thereafter, though not aloud.

Diverse Piccolomini, Renaissance man
Before Castiglione or *The Prince*,
Or rising anti-Trinitarian
Disturbances, or Leonardo's tints
Teasing our gaze for meaning ever since,
Having, on elevation, set to work
Against Catilinarians and the Turk

TO AENIUS SILVIUS ON MONTE AMIATA

With Quattrocento clarity, what relief,
Despite intrigues and venomous ill wills
And plans for coalition come to grief,
Plus torment from the gout, and other ills,
Carried by litter over the Tuscan hills,
You felt at ease in Amiata's shade
Beneath chestnuts and oaks, where sunlight played

Tricks of perspective on the studious eye
Marking beyond the steep declivity
Siena's towers against the cobalt sky
(You couldn't climb up to the top to see
Distant Sardinia lifting off the sea),
Finding yourself, peaceful against all hope,
That contradictory thing, a happy Pope.

✥

DR. JOHNSON ROLLS DOWN A HILL

Even a man of voluminous gravity,
The monumental lexicographer
Who labored in inconvenience and distraction,
In sorrow, sickness, and slovenly poverty
Unaided by the learned or the great,
A man of girth and passionate appetite
Who relished with dispatch and enormous zest
Huge stacks of pancakes, bottomless pots of tea,
Along with whatever conversational thrust
Kept the mind nimble and the spirit light,
Delaying the final, agonizing hour
When he lumbered off to bed, always alone,
To self-recrimination in pitch dark,
Contains in his heart of hearts a little boy
Who played and played all day, without a thought
Of duty or expectation or penury
Or wasted years diminishing all the time.

Not to idealize childhood, least of all his:
Barely alive at birth, too weak to cry,
Infected in infancy by tubercular milk,
Rendered half blind, half deaf, with an open wound
Stitched in his little arm for his first six years
(An issue, with so much else, he learned to ignore),
Scarred by the scrofula, and further scarred
By being cut sans anesthesia,
He wasn't a pretty sight, but bore it all,
The constant pain, the perpetual awkwardness,
The fretting of parents, and the feckless taunts
Of boys who could play ball and ridicule
The rawboned, driveling prodigy in their midst,
And grew to be a man of great physical strength
Despite his pitiful incapacities.

The body had its struggles. So did the mind.
The photographic memory, the sheer
Celerity and clarity and taut

DR. JOHNSON ROLLS DOWN A HILL

Engagement with the question, small or large,
Be it some pressing affair of state, or some
Domestic crisis pressing upon the heart
Of one he loved, encompassing his point
With honesty and syntax and good sense,
Such gifts the mind deployed with bravery
While poised above a vertiginous abyss
Opening wide within, a whirligig
Of deep afflictions and anxieties:
Depression, sloth, despair, paralysis,
An "inward hostility against himself"
In which his massive critical faculty
Would pulverize his puny self-regard,
And, worst of all, pure terror at the dark
Encroachments of what seemed insanity.

Now, in his middle fifties, the shadows lengthen,
"A kind of strange oblivion" overspreads him.
Beset by horrors and perplexities,
The clicks and spasms and clucking of Tourette's
Markedly worsen as the great man sinks
Deeper in torpor, till guilt at time misspent
Freezes and harrows him, transfixed, become
A spectator at his own stunned debacle,
Tortured by scruples like pebbles in his shoes.
He's written nothing for years, and Shakespeare waits,
Promised and paid for but beyond him still
(What infinite riches, and what little room),
As vast resources of intelligence
Fritter away from faulty "character,"
And reason flickers, dying, all but snuffed
Out by the listless drift of hopelessness.
His friends try to distract him, to little avail,
With a club, a trip to the country, anything ...

He visits Lincolnshire with Bennet Langton
In January 1764.

DR. JOHNSON ROLLS DOWN A HILL

He's on his best behavior, charming both
His young friend's parents and their visitors.
One fine, dry afternoon, windless and clear,
They set out walking on the Lincolnshire wolds.
Only the groundsel's in bloom, a tentative yellow,
As they amble past tufts of grouse scrub, furze, and thorn,
But the air has a pleasing crispness, with a rich,
Effluvial hint of leaf-mold or of wood-rot.
The hills are varied by streaks of yellowish red
Which vaguely correspond to, lower down,
The low, red roofs of occasional cottages.
Everything's very still. There are just three birds:
A fluttering brace of fieldfares (or are they redwings?),
Plus a lone kestrel, hovering for a vole.

They reach the top of an impressive hill.
Admiring its steepness, suddenly Johnson declares
He has "not had a roll for a long time."
Against the objections of the company
He divests himself of pencil, keys, and purse,
Lies down at the edge, and, after a turn
Or two, is off and tumbling and picking up speed
Flattening the flora in his path
While sending up puffs of chalk dust, now he's chuckling
As his weight propels him and his heaviness
Precipitating his new view revolves
As sky and earth wheel round in blue-brown circles
And happiness is merely being alive,
As if the good life really were this easy,
As if the nightmare of his coming breakdown
Had no more substance than a child's bad dream.

HENRI PROVENCE IN WESSEX

Now, when the thatch-roofed cottages
    Send up their puffs and curls
From heating folk and pottages,
    And steadily thickening swirls

Of snow-feathers settle, limning
    Lintels and mullioned panes,
And door lanterns waver, dimming,
    And rusty weather vanes

Creak as they flip directions like
    Befuddled gyroscopes,
A chilling bleakness seems to strike
    Down all too human hopes

For what the year now past would bring
    And how our lives would change,
Before our goals for everything
    Had drifted out of range

(Time set aside for self-improvement
    Got taken up like slack;
The old inertias stymied movement;
    She never called you back).

When I, to see what prevents me,
    Go blundering outside,
The blank the winter presents me
    Scintillates far and wide

With all distinct articulation
    Of coppice, hedge, and heather
Erased in glazed disanimation
    By all-encasing weather

HENRI PROVENCE IN WESSEX

That levels whatever playing field
    We thought the game was on,
And levels us, who stand revealed
    As going, if not gone.

An influence presents itself
    Where all this absence is,
As if one old book on my shelf
    Inscribed precisely this,

As if down an empty country lane
    I saw Thomas Hardy go,
Ghosting the track of some whitened pain
    Like boot-prints filled by snow.

LARKIN'S NEPHEW

"I don't believe you're not on Facebook yet,"
    The bubbly poet said.
"I put everything up there, who I've met
    And where, what I've just read

Or had for lunch. People appreciate
    Knowing, they really do.
It helps us all keep so in touch—it's great!
    It'd work real well for you.

All your old friends could find you then, from high
    School, right online. You never
Know who might pop up next and just say 'hi.'
    It's like the best thing ever."

Somehow I'm not persuaded. It makes less sense
    To let the great net work
If you're like me. Flashbacks to adolescence?
    To times I was a jerk

Playing elaborate jokes on some dumb schmuck
    Who never stood a chance?
That guy might track me down now—just my luck.
    My hot date to the dance?

I didn't have one, ever. Can't I please
    Keep on forgetting years
Sullied by acne and anxiety's
    Clammy pubescent fears?

I will admit I've sometimes been curious
    What happened to two or three
Young women on whom my crush was furious.
    But they never cared for me.

OH

When Love herself came to me
Framed by the classroom door
Her presence shot straight through me,
My heart dropped to the floor.

Nothing phantasmal slew me.
What eyes and hair and skin
Could do they did to do me,
Helpless and hopeless, in.

Oh when her news came to me
—Ovarian, forty-four—
Her absence echoed through me,
Ringing my hollowed core.

✝

SUNDAY EVENING

The night is clear, without the slightest wind,
As the moon poses her soft white proposition
Above the plaza and the rooftop gardens.
Even the mountains are visible on the horizon
As jagged pieces sliced from the rim of the sky.
Sweetheart, the streets are quiet, a few windows
Reflect the lives still taking place by lamplight
Or the blue flickering of a television.
You are asleep now, in your chic apartment,
Perhaps alone, perhaps not, having cancelled,
Politely but firmly, our long awaited evening,
Pleading fatigue. And last night *was* a party.
I'd say you looked your best, but every time
I think you do the next time you look better,
Which makes things worse, and worse they may be yet,
For who's to say your best's not still to come?
Not me, who hope I won't be there to see it
And pray I will, or all those other fellows
Who cleverly compete for your attention
While I observe your triumph from a distance
Across the room that might be miles, or years.

Speaking of years, who now reads Leopardi,
Or Keats, or Shelley, or even Wallace Stevens?
You used to. Now you haven't got the time,
And I can't say I blame you. They're not changing.
What's new is fast and all the buzz and edgy.
What, really, is the point of antique passions
—An oxymoron if there ever was one—
Except to pluck the classical guitar strings
Of melancholics' overripe nostalgias?
Names that once conjured worlds mean little today.
The evening's silence seems a comment on them
Like lapses in attention, and if a poem
Somebody wrote two hundred years ago
Informs the space your absence opens here
(It stretches all the way to Recanati)

SUNDAY EVENING

Would anybody know unless I told them?
And now the silence suddenly gets broken,
Ruptured by woofers, and an engine revving,
And high-heeled, tipsy laughter clacking home,
Sounds sharpening the ache of the outsider
Who hears the young world rushing on without him.

When I was a little boy in Alabama
I used to lie awake on Sunday evenings.
The weekend I had waited for was over,
And why was I so sad? The Fifth Dimension
Sang somewhere on a crackling radio
About the dawning age of constellations
Or something. I couldn't tell. But I did know
There was some big thing happening without me
And I would always live with having missed it.
I was born just too late, and missed the Sixties,
Though not the sense the world had changed completely
In ways I couldn't wrap my head around
That somehow got embodied in the music.
I didn't know why what I felt inside me
Tugged and tangled and wound itself up into
A giant knot of unrelieved frustration
So dolorous I sobbed into my pillow.
The dull school days ahead (I hated school),
Insipid as institutional architecture,
Kept stretching off as far as I could see.
I knew the music hurt me. It still does,
Dying off bit by bit in memory,
Even tonight, at my age, to the core.

✝

THE SITE

Welcome to the site. There is no need
For you to furnish personal information,
Financial or otherwise. We have all that
Already in your file, which activated
The moment you logged on, and contains, as well,
Full documentation of errors you've long forgotten,
Early embarrassments, rank ineptitudes
You've wiped your record clean of, but not ours,
Humiliations suffered and meted out,
Crass self-indulgence, curt ingratitude,
The outright frauds, the sinuous lies left in,
All catalogued, were there reason to produce
Evidence in the course of these proceedings.

Cooperation is, you will admit,
The best route, not to say the only one.
You have a simple password now required
For everything. To form it, just insert
Your name and date of birth into the code
"JohnDoe060666thefool."
Should you ever be forced to leave your screen
For longer than the standard daily allowance
(Three twenty-minute breaks, six hours at night)
By medical emergency or fire,
Or receive a privilege day of personal leave
To attend a funeral or consult a surgeon,
You'll need it to log back on and resume your life.

Here is your list of friends. A few you know,
A few know you, most of them we've selected
Using compatibility algorithms.
Here is your pictorial representation,
The eyes, the hair, the smile by which you'll be
Identified as you from this day forward.
Better, you must admit, than you as you were,
And all who love you will be happy you
Look as they could have wished you all along.

THE SITE

We trust you will not fail to recognize
This altogether flattering transformation
As one more reason not to leave your screen.

Not that you'll ever want to. Virtually
Every form of entertainment is here
At finger-tip control: travel the world
To jungle, reef, savannah, glacial peak
Swept over in 3D, with background music
From our extensive ... well, you get the picture.
Plus videos, movies, concerts, galleries, sports,
Books graphic and otherwise, perpetual parties,
Family reunions, all here: just see the menu.
And the games, of course. The games go on and on,
Fast and violent all the way up the ladder
And ratcheting effects to boost you again.
We've signed you up for all the latest versions.

These are the only available arrangements.
You understand, we think. Of course. We thought so.
Deactivate your will with just a keystroke.

THE KEY

Here is the key. The lock is on the door
Of a small cabin in a distant wood
Standing for something you've never understood,
An emptiness that's full of metaphor.

Assembly *is* required. Don't mind the score,
It's minding you. You might have known it would
Be all attention, taking your measure for good
Like the complaining boards of a warping floor.

The key's in your pocket, hot as the summer sky
Baking the city you left years ago.
The streets forgot your absence, by and by.

Here it's darkening. Soon it's going to snow.
Then the brilliant cover, the perfect lie
Telling what little truth you've come to know.

THE PLACE

You'll never find the place, but you must try.
Start on a rain-lashed, storm-tormented night,
Driven by gusts and gales in stark-blind flight
(Instructions for navigation are a lie).
Come day, the landscape gives you the evil eye
From every angle's freshly hideous sight

Of blasted, strip-mined hillsides, curdled pools
Radiating an unnatural sheen
From surfaces of foam-fringed, toxic green.
A foul smell drifts in noxious molecules.
What dismal game, played by what dirty rules,
Contrived to bring you to this blistered scene,

Dragging your damaged sensibility
To what bad end? A permanent eclipse,
Whether it's pre- or post-apocalypse,
Surrounding you as far as you can see
In random mounds of dirt, gravel, and scree,
Of what you thought the world was? The worst trips

Of nightmare, or psychedelia gone wrong,
Were larks compared to this infernal fix.
The lines of dead trees stand like burnt matchsticks
Up the next valley, where you trudge along
The brown, cracked dryness of a billabong.
The very ground, like malformed cicatrix,

Looks traumatized, infected. You push on
To climb, at last, onto a barren plain
(What bitter labor for what dubious gain)
Of gray cement. What engineers, long gone,
Laid out this space from which all life's withdrawn?
What overlords required such dead domain?

THE PLACE

A place without inflection, ornament,
Or variation: every inch the same,
Now nameless, if there even was a name
For all its single-minded bleak intent.
What creatures lived here dully came and went
Without a remnant, if they ever came.

And yet you cross it, somehow, to arrive
At a vast tract of ugly, uniform
Apartment buildings. Whatever spies inform
The premises, not one thing seems alive
In these dull eyesores ranged in groups of five,
Stuck in adherence to some stupid norm.

Beyond them, you encounter a huge mass
Of crushed, wrenched metal, twisted, tortured piles
Of scrap, abandoned, stretching on for miles,
All rust and wreckage. Crunching broken glass
You pick your way around each sharp impasse
To stagger on in search of other trials.

Waste land after waste land! And all man-made,
Or man-destroyed, civilization's crux
And crucible, matter itself redux
As pure detritus, while we masquerade
Pretending we were dealt the hand we played,
We who have seen the future, and it sucks.

Don't go there? How? Perverse euphoria,
To revel in such grand guignol grotesque,
Or scribble pornographic arabesque
To decorate phantasmagoria!
Social dementia's our aporia,
The end we've earned. For *this* you left your desk?

THE PLACE

But in a flash the whole scene's morphed again:
There's grass, though withered, and a furtive stream
With a trickle or two of water, and what would seem
A clump of stunted trees, gnarled as in pain,
And hills (not mountains) ringing a little plain
Which looks familiar, maybe from a dream,

Or from a poem. Oh. This is the place.
Why didn't you, you old fool, recognize
Its round, squat truth against the ground of lies
You've crossed and recrossed, lugging the carapace
That can't protect you now? The prize you chase
Will turn on you and cut you down to size.

A bell tolls, once. You're back in time. You stand
Surrounded by a winding sheet of flame.
They see and know you, and you hear your name
Repeated mockingly, your corpus panned
As failed at failure, who crashed *Alastor*, and
Who blew "'Childe Roland to the Dark Tower Came.'"

✥

SPARSE RHYMES

"O poverella mia, come se' rozza!"

When I was a young man
I was like a little child
Who, desperate to speak, has not yet learned
To make the sounds he can
Hear, and it drives him wild.
Frustrated, flummoxed, I kept on getting burned
Whenever the urge returned
To finally be heard,
The heart on my sleeve a joke
Your laughter sent up in smoke,
My stammers marring every perfect word,
My tongue just in the way
Of all I tried to say.

When I at least attained
A basic fluency
I thought you'd love me. Every undertaking
Set out with mind's eye trained
On your eyes fixed on me,
Not on the road straight uphill I was taking.
I was, of course, mistaking
Your interest all the time
In what could only bore,
My stiff attempts to score
With reams of thudding rhythm, gorgeous rhyme.
For proof I was deluded
Reality intruded

SPARSE RHYMES

      As your demurrals came
      Rocketing back by post.
I wasn't, really, someone *you* could date,
      Recipient of a name
      Rejected coast to coast,
The late beginner who began too late.
      Call it bad luck, or fate,
      Or instrumental flaw:
      Although I felt maligned
      (Your notes weren't even signed),
Selection picks. The law is just the law.
      Dislike is natural
      Where love's ephemeral.

      And when I turned more hip
      (Farewell academy,
Hello café: why *not* performance art?)
      You still gave me the slip
      With deft celerity.
I conned myself into another part:
      You, prompted, broke my heart
      Along with our appointment,
      Infinite expectation
      Just hallucination.
The gadget broke, the fly stuck in the ointment
      As yet another stage
      Got flattened by the page.

SPARSE RHYMES

    As someone bad at poker
    Who keeps on losing hands
Will once, right when he needs it, draw the ace
    (Or was it just the joker?)
    He hardly understands
Will serve to keep him, losing, in his place,
    One time I saw your face
    And you *did* smile. I'd scored
    Big, in the nick of time
    The cards lined up like rhyme
And here you came, and out my winnings poured
    In brilliant, brief success
    That paid off less and less.

    You long since stripped me clean.
    These days my instrument
Makes harsh sounds only, as befits my age.
    I shrink from anything green
    And full of all that meant,
The hearts on ice, the diamond equipage.
    At my diminished stage
    I simply watch you stroll,
    As if the world were yours
    For parties and grand tours,
Out with the latest stylist on a roll,
    Or sometimes, down by the water,
    Playing with your daughter,

SPARSE RHYMES

   Reminding me of ... no.
   We'll leave some things unsaid.
Inside a place we called the Forest of Arden
   We walked once, long ago.
   You barely moved your head,
Your voice was faint, you vaguely begged my pardon.
   I felt my proud heart harden.
   So it went, and always would.
   What rhymes I have I scatter
   Wherever they least matter,
Here where we walked that evening. If I could
   I'd sing you one last song
   But fear I'd get it wrong.

   Little song, you know you're no good.
   Better stay here in the wood.

✠

ARCHIBALD LEACH

Archibald Leach was the perfect leading man
Who had that *je ne sais quoi* you can't teach.
His dapper smarts and rapid-fire élan
Were signature, but not signed Archibald Leach.

Men mimicked his clip and polish. To the girls
He was dreamy as ice cream sundaes at the beach.
But who, adoring his picture, reciting his pearls,
Knew that the man with that view was Archibald Leach?

Granted he carried the day, whatever the name
Considered for awards just out of reach.
The credits keep on rolling just the same.
But credit is never given to Archibald Leach.

HE WASN'T PROUST

In London, on his birthday, he went to a play
That seemed a good bet: Helen Mirren in *Phèdre*.
He thought it unlikely he would be disappointed,
Or crushed if he were: he wasn't Marcel Proust.
And this was no reprise—for her the role was new.
What were the chances *she* would be underpowered?

But her performance was, well, underpowered.
Though he was rather impressed with the rest of the play,
The staging, the acting, even the verse, he knew
Its star had fallen short (too old for Phèdre?),
Straining, like an aging character in Proust,
At a forced passion. Mildly disappointed,

He was disturbed he wasn't more disappointed.
His own reaction was, well, underpowered.
Why couldn't he, like young Marcel in Proust,
Feel crucified by art? At his first play,
Anticipating his favorite part of *Phèdre*,
When "Berma" would sound the deepest speech he knew,

"On dit qu'un prompt départ vous éloigne de nous,"
He was so devastatingly disappointed!
His dream of dreams, to see "Berma" as Phèdre,
Was ruined: her voice was flat and underpowered.
He didn't have the experience of the play
He'd always imagined. He was already Proust,

If years from being a character in Proust.
Perhaps all this would get *him* to write something new.
Not a sestina. For even when you play
Some high cards well, the reader is disappointed.
The teleutons turn mechanical, underpowered.
How many times can a poem mention *Phèdre*

HE WASN'T PROUST

And not be seeming to strain to work in "*Phèdre*"?
How many times can a poem bring up Proust?
On reflection, the whole idea seemed underpowered,
Thin, predictable, certainly nothing new.
Better not try at all than be disappointed.
So that was that. There was nothing to overplay,

Or under-. Powered down, and out, he knew
He wouldn't write about *Phèdre*. He wasn't Proust.
But he *was* disappointed, though not with the play.

PORTRAIT OF THE ARTIST AS A YOUNG KID

There they were in the basement, the whole troop
    Of Cub Scouts, including his brothers,
    Instructed by attending mothers
In projects spread out on the ping-pong table
    Right at eye level (he was five
        And out of the loop),
      Where he could, barely, see
      A jumbled activity
      He was unable
To join line up and come alive,
    As each initiate was shown
How to fold a *Reader's Digest* into a cone,
    Which soon, spray-painted green
    Then sprinkled with glitter and cotton strands
(And just like that somebody's life expands:
    Was this the coolest thing he'd seen?),
      Emerged from their clumsy hands
        A Christmas tree.
      What strange, imagined lands,
        What inner sea

Right then conceived their dark geography
    And left the issued world behind,
    Their black maps rising in his mind?
What territories, perilous and wild,
    Whose powers would demand oblation,
        Then came to be,
      In firmaments apart,
      The regions of his heart?
        The scheming child
    (Always beyond representation)
    Had a vague notion what to do:
He made, with cotton balls and Elmer's glue,
    A shapeless pile of gloop
    Proudly affixing to the floor
Off in a corner behind the basement door.
    So what he wasn't in the group?

PORTRAIT OF THE ARTIST AS A YOUNG KID

He'd seen what life was for
    And made a start.
This thing was his, and more:
    It was his art.

✠

DAMON

"Go, for they call you, shepherd, from the hills."
Untie your charges, set their figures, penned
With all due caution for the present time,
Loose to consider what the signs intend
In fields of play star-dazzled, fringed with rime.
    They have their own free wills,
And they will wander, under a harvest moon,
Into predicaments you can't foresee
Where passages drop into history
Implicit in a word. Let it be soon.

Here, where some upland gardener planned the rows
And laid them out in, oh, two dozen plots
To make a statement through the sun and rain
With poppies, blue-bells, and forget-me-nots
(Whether such style will work this spot again
    Nobody living knows),
Here where the footing's tricky, the ground steep,
And no one comes now but the occasional poor
Student who can't tell what the place was for,
While most folk, docile, stay below, like sheep

But less adventurous, I sit and wait
To see what comes along. The view is quite
Romantic, one might say: the valley swerves
Down with the river's ribbon glinting light,
The hills stand forested in gentle curves,
    And though it's getting late
The trees still have their leaves, although they've turned
To rust and umber and alizarin
As cold, precise as clockwork, zeroes in
To teach them what their ancestors all learned,

DAMON

A dyeing fall. Pencilled against the blue,
The Gothic spires of the academy
Compete with the church steeples of the town
For altitude and what antiquity
This stage set offers, till the sun draws down
    The curtain, with much ado
Of lighting effects on a spectacular scale.
Till then, to pass time in this pastoral nook
I've bread, cheese, wine, and Matthew Arnold's book,
So I can read, once more, that wandering tale

Of the lone scholar who forsook his friends
And Oxford's citadel of inquiry
Along established lines, in scripted parts,
To choose a life of constant errancy
In search of ancient gnosis and dark arts
    For mesmerizing ends,
And disappeared into the landscape, hill
And field and tree turned signs of his vanishing,
His present absence, his self-banishing
In rigors of conjuration and wicked skill.

I know, my friend, what that poem brings to mind
For both of us: that character we knew
Some twenty years ago, when we were first
Trying to write more seriously, who
Would startle us with each rhapsodic burst.
    Fearless, one of a kind,
A learned enthusiast, a mad-cap bard,
He had entire anthologies by heart:
You couldn't stop him once you'd let him start.
His poems were densely coded, and too hard

DAMON

For us to make much of. But we still thought
Something was going on there, for we heard
A different resonance, a pitch and key
Animating each encrypted word
With overtones of strange authority,
    Compelling and self-taught.
Try to advise him and he'd have none of it.
Tell him to let some air in, tone it down,
Just meet the reader halfway, he would frown
And scoff at compromise: he was above it.

He criticized *us*: we were stuck in time,
Attuned to the present moment, unaware
Of spectral pressures, unextinguished sparks
And ghostly demarcations, the very air
Swarming with presences, invisible marks
    At the scene of each new crime
Telling just whom we'd robbed. Our ignorance
Was no excuse. Trap doors in every trope
Dropped into the abyss. There was no hope
For dancers who couldn't sense the larger dance.

Then he was gone, dropped out of school and sight.
For a while we heard about him, knocking around,
Performing in cafés, or giving classes
In bookstore basements. Stories had him found
Haunting the alleys and the underpasses,
    A rag-tag anchorite
Reading to rats and winos. It wasn't pretty.
Soon he was homeless, living out of his car,
Strung out on dope, cracked up, locked up, or far
Gone down the vicious sinkhole of the city.

DAMON

Or somehow he'd escaped his downward spiral.
He was squatting in a vacant barn in Sparks
And renting fishing boats on Pretty Boy.
He'd nabbed an airstream and was living in parks
In West Virginia. He was peddling soy
    Butter and antiviral
Herbal remedies on the Eastern Shore.
Now he was teaching yoga in Delaware.
He was all rumor, he was everywhere
And nowhere fast. Then we heard nothing more.

I do still think I see him, now and then.
On cliffs across the river at Great Falls,
Up a side street in Chelsea, walking fast,
As trains pull out of stations, at last calls,
When faces blend as crowds come pouring past
    I glimpse, time and again,
Reflections of who he was, or might be now,
Those deep-set gray-green eyes that look right through
Whatever public face you think is you
To size up just what you've become, and how.

At times I even think we made him up,
Or plucked some fellow out of history
To serve as foil and proxy, and explore
Precincts too marginal for you or me,
Beer stubes and rum dives of old Baltimore,
    To drain one final cup
Of some cheap, foul, nightmare-inducing stuff
And stagger off half-crazy, and then go
Roaming the streets with Edgar Allan Poe,
Agreed too much was never quite enough.

DAMON

But that was life, or death. It was, of course,
In art that we admired his recklessness,
His upward swerving purpose, his conviction
That more was really more, and less just less,
His labyrinthine syntax, loaded diction,
    And fence-clearing high horse.
He knew the back trails through the mountain passes,
The sequences of all the trees and flowers,
Where caved-in grottoes were, and ruined towers.
He, clearly, saw it all. We wore dark glasses.

(Or blinkers. Was he right in getting out
Before it got to him, remaining pure-
Ly idiosyncratic? He didn't settle
For some entitled quasi-sinecure.
His touchstone leaves its mark on our cheap metal
    Dented by fear and doubt,
Security assured yet insecure.)
He's out there somewhere strange, insistently
Striding beyond reliance, cast off, free,
Trying to read the secretive signature

Of things to come, as in a glass reflected.
Spotting the cruise ships of the new regime
He fled the hoops and hoopla, traps and trends
And smug correction by the episteme,
Spurned colloquy and group-appointed ends,
    And, proudly self-elected,
Crossed the great gulf solo, lowered his sails,
Like some Tyrian trader set up shop
Sans network, sans connection, sans laptop,
"And on the beach undid his corded bales."

TO RICCARDO DURANTI

Vides ut alta stet nive candida Soracte ...

My friend Riccardo, you are a lucky fellow
To have a hilltop farm in the Sabine hills
Where you raise olives and figs and lettuces
And live with your eager dog and a couple of cats.
A wise man, too, to leave the city behind
And give up teaching down there and work from home,
Translating poems and novels and whatever you like.

You've built an airy new house out of old stone
On the old spot. It's modest, but ample, too,
Fit for your purpose and friendly to visitors.
Even quite ancient things can be put to new use,
Becoming timeless and contemporary.
Conglomerate, limestone, and *sponga* have served you well,
As well as they served your ancestors way back when.

On days when a cool wind combs the leaves of your elms
And ripples your split-by-lightning mulberry,
And the jasmine your mother planted as a girl
Billows and luffs like the hopes of the very young
For whom every season is fresh and the hours move slowly,
As a caravan of clouds casts Salisano
Continually in and out of light and shadow
You can still see, in the distance, Mount Soratte,
Just as the poet did from a different angle
When it was inches taller and covered in snow.

Who needs an apartment in Rome when you have all this?
Who needs to be sipping Giacchè or Amarone
When the *rosso* your cousin Spartaco provides
Comes in huge jugs and gets better the more you drink it?

Although I believe this poem should tell you something,
Any advice I might give you would be superfluous;
You're already living the way I would urge you to.
I can only think of a single, trivial warning:

TO RICCARDO DURANTE

Beware of your nasty old neighbor down the road.
He cheats at pool like a little Berlusconi.

TO BARACK OBAMA

You've written me, once again, to ask for money.
I thought I would send you, as well, a little advice,
In nearly perfect confidence it won't reach you.

My father used to exclaim, when one of his children
Was frustrated by human stupidity,
By prejudice, or envy, or petty meanness,
"Don't let the dungheads get you down!" It helped
A bit, perhaps since when he said it, he always
Let loose a hearty belly laugh, in pure
Pleasure at his own sanguine, salty proverb,
Which never left him, however often he found
Occasion to trot it out with his great guffaw,
Even in rather embarrassing circumstances,
As one of my sisters, for instance, was nervously lurching
Off to some tittering rendezvous with her friends
Who were standing there, bewildered, well within hearing.

I imagine you don't. How could you? You wouldn't have time.
For some of us, though, watching all this can be tough,
As much of the country believes you're trouble incarnate,
Mao and Malcolm and Gogmagog rolled into one,
And others are deeply, miserably disappointed
Your presidency has been, of course, imperfect,
And you haven't solved most of our problems the way they'd hoped.
But given the metacrises you were given—
An economy in the tank and two wars on,
With shameless opposition whose loyalties
Attend on their donors and party before their country—
It seems to me so far you've done rather well,
And I think it will look that way in the long perspective
(Poets do take the long view: it's all we've got).

And while I have your metaphorical ear,
I thought I would include these rough translations
Of Florentine maxims from the Renaissance:

TO BARACK OBAMA

Too much reliance on a comfort circle
Of loyal friends has scuppered many a prince.

Your enemies are as ruthless as they are foolish
Concerning all the issues that matter most.

The cautious man may miss the safest path.

When you inherit a hopeless enterprise,
Doing the things that might have made a difference
Back when a difference was still there to be made
Doesn't make any difference.

To escape the Cyclops' cave you have to blind him.

This comes to you with only admiration.
You carry an epic burden, and carry it nobly.
Please give my best to Michelle, a wonderful lady.
I'm enclosing, along with this poem, a modest check.

TO HIS BOOK

You seem to want, my book, to be out on our own,
Imagining the world will be eager to greet you,
Will applaud the panache of your various moods and meters
And ponder the counterpoint of your arrangement.

Children don't listen to parents, or else I would tell you
To temper your expectations, or chuck them entirely.
I doubt you will find yourself dodging the paparazzi,
Or getting invited to all the most glamorous parties,
Or making the short lists. Not that you won't deserve to.
But you're built for distance, not for the sprints to prizes.

My hope for you is that the handful of readers
Who admired your older brothers will like you better,
And another dozen or two will happen across you
And feel compelled to riddle out where you come from.
Everything else is gravy, though welcome, of course.

If they ask you about me, tell them whatever you like.
The truth won't help, and lies won't hurt in the long run.

I know you were hoping for some extravagant send-off.
But at least I didn't compare you to a donkey,
Or a prostitute, or a senile grade-school teacher.

I am not, though, putting this last, where you think it belongs.

TO TREBITSCH LINCOLN IN HELL

Where in Hell would Dante Alighieri
Stick you, what torments laced with fire or ice
Would he inflict, how far down would he bury

A connoisseur of almost every vice,
A flimflam man, a thief, a cad, a spy,
A peddler of false hopes and bad advice

Whose penchant for the shameless, bold-faced lie
Consorted with delusional fantasy
From Montreal to Munich to Shanghai

In a career straining credulity,
Who kept on popping up in some odd spot
Like the bad penny of the century

Wherever scoundrels with a half-baked plot
Could cause more trouble, adding your two bits
To further snarl your life tale's tangled knot

Of false identities and nutty fits
And harebrained stunts to plump your empty purse
By conning chumps and chumming up to shits,

Of making dicey situations worse
Through hazardous addiction to foul play
And megalomania? You were a curse

To anyone you met along the way
You took to infamy, whose antics crammed
A bulging Foreign Office dossier

(What clowns you bothered, and what fools you scammed!)
With puzzlement and mounting irritation,
Annoyance typed and scrawled and telegrammed

TO TREBITSCH LINCOLN IN HELL

In disbelief and crusty indignation
At squabbles, crimes, political intrigue,
Another hapless passport application,

Caustic dismissals, threats of something big
From a preposterous hallucinating
Sham operator in unlikely league

With fascist thugs and dictators-in-waiting,
Tapping an endless reservoir of schemes
To feed your wounded, vengeful, unabating

Procession of world domination dreams,
Absurd yet dangerous malignancies
Envisioning despicable regimes

In strange alignment, all so you could seize
Power somewhere somehow. Your gall amazes
Anyone who, examining the lees

Of right-wing politics, the clueless mazes
Of failed conspiracies, keeps finding you,
And tracks your progress through its baffling phases:

Born on the Danube, a Hungarian Jew;
Then a failed thespian; a jewel thief;
A fugitive; a journalist; a Lu-

Theran seminarian (this stint was brief);
A missionary who received the call
To carve out and exploit a petty fief

Converting the stubborn Jews of Montreal
(Not one converted), then quit, demanding more
Compensation for your theatrical

TO TREBITSCH LINCOLN IN HELL

Evangelizing (if your results were poor,
Your self-regard was only growing greater);
A curate in the parish of Appledore

Terminated rather sooner than later
When you flunked ordination horribly;
A secretary and social investigator

Studying Belgium as the employee
Of your most generous, trusting benefactor,
The cocoa potentate Seebohm Rowntree,

For whom you served as brash and hasty factor,
Brandishing the cause of land reform
To prove a pompous nuisance and bad actor

Badgering functionaries to perform
Unnecessary favors, which got done
Despite resentment fueled by brutal form;

A Liberal MP for Darlington
(Some dogs will have their day, despite their fleas),
Having astonished almost everyone

By nipping the incumbent, H. Pike Pease,
Against the tide, who soon became a joke,
A swaggering backbencher little cheese

Whose accent triggered jibes both times he spoke
(You were irrelevant, but you were loud:
Your vehement posturing managed to provoke

A caricature in *Punch*, which you were proud
To show off from then on, wherever you went),
And under party pressure and a cloud

TO TREBITSCH LINCOLN IN HELL

Of soaring debt and wide embarrassment
Was finally persuaded to stand down
After a single year in Parliament

Of meretricious service to both crown
And country (which were *not* free of you yet:
You weren't one to lie low, or just skip town);

A speculator who contrived to get
Investors and East European counts
To back your shifty and untimely bet

On oil bonanzas with quite large amounts
Of capital, despite clear signs of trouble
(Shell companies and vanishing accounts:

Confronting losses, you would always double
Down), at the ill-fated Oil and Drilling Trust
Of Roumania, which rode the next oil bubble

But not for long, then went, predictably, bust,
Leaving you once again in poverty
If somehow free from prosecution, just;

A bald practitioner of forgery,
Signing, when new creditors demanded
A guarantor, the name "Seebohm Rowntree"

To missives of assurance, a trick which landed
You in a little down time, by and by;
A postal censor who got reprimanded

For writing *on* the letters, and in high
Dudgeon at such treatment walked out the door;
A self-denominated "master spy"

TO TREBITSCH LINCOLN IN HELL

Trying to work both sides in the Great War
(The Germans nibbled, the Brits would not play ball,
Which left you apoplectic, with a score

To settle with your bête noir, "Blinker" Hall,
A twitch-afflicted naval officer
Who sized your act up and saw through it all

To you, a shameless, fraudulent character
Who'd sold what soul he had, and long ago);
An on-the-lam shipboard adulterer

Lining up crash pads and, of course, cash flow
In your next stop, New York, where you would try
To peddle your latest dog and pony show,

Poking the hated British in the eye
With scandalous articles and your first book,
Revelations of an International Spy,

Trumpeting treason, which was all it took
To land you, as you preened and celebrated
Celebrity, back, firmly, on the hook

(With a war on, this really could have waited)
Of those fraud charges, cause to extradite
And get you, at long last, incarcerated,

At first in Brooklyn (you put up a fight,
And managed to escape, and then get caught),
Then Parkhurst Prison on the Isle of Wight

For three dull years, a punishment that taught
You absolutely nothing—no restrictions
Could interrupt your fuming, overwrought

TO TREBITSCH LINCOLN IN HELL

Propensity for self-propelling fictions,
Which led you off more cliffs, as we shall see;
An ex-con who, with Anglophobe convictions,

Sought restoration of the monarchy
In Germany, and to promote that cause
Courted Prince Wilhelm in the Zuider Zee

(He wouldn't see you); an ally of scofflaws
And militarists intent on snatching power
(That you were Jewish gave these friends some pause)

Like Ludendorff and Erhardt and Max Bauer
And Wolfgang Kapp, who gave the putsch its name
That seized Berlin for a proverbial hour

(Well, five days, really) to abruptly flame
Out in confusion, buckling under the stress
Of crummy players at a dirty game,

And smack dab in the middle of this mess
There *you* were, putting on ridiculous airs
To bully and browbeat the foreign press

As, yes, Director of Foreign Press Affairs,
And as that house of cards began to fall
You did pass Adolf Hitler on the stairs;

A founder of that virulent cabal
Of cancerous revanchist fantasy,
The sinister White International,

A festering wingnut conspiracy
Nursed in Bavaria and Budapest
Committed to fomenting anomie

TO TREBITSCH LINCOLN IN HELL

And unifying hatred of the West
That never managed to metastasize,
For all your grotesque zeal and evil zest;

A desperate turncoat, having gotten wise
To plans among your "friends" to snuff you out,
And taken off with a trove of compromis-

Ing documents, which wares you shopped about,
Approaching the French, the English, and the Czechs
With tales of right-wing plotting, which no doubt

Contained exaggerations and complex
Evasions, but for once were basically true,
Though no one would accept those purloined specs

As genuine, because they came from you;
An aid to *Chinese* forces of reaction,
Advisor to Yang Sen and Wu P'ei-fu

And other warlords of the Chihli faction,
Who guided a fund-raising carnival
To Europe on their behalf (which gained no traction);

An arms dealer, perhaps; a professional
Gambler, who thought he knew a way to win
At baccarat (you didn't); a tell-all

Purveyor of your heroics (this had worn thin);
The blessed recipient of revelation
At the Astor House Hotel in Tientsin,

Who then embraced "the great renunciation"
And "quit the world" (just momentarily)
In search of spiritual elevation,

TO TREBITSCH LINCOLN IN HELL

And, after a brief fling with Theosophy,
Retreated to a Buddhist monastery
On Ceylon, where, in proud humility,

You contemplated truth; a missionary
And roving lecturer raptly expounding
Buddhist doctrine to various unwary

Audiences, somehow involved in founding
A center for enlightenment in San
Francisco (thought the first); again confounding

All expectation, a certified holy man,
Having gone through initiation rites
To be branded and ordained at Pao-hua Shan,

Near Nanking, who ascended greater heights,
Quickly clambering up another rung
From monk to *Bodhisattva*, and by such lights

You were henceforth the Venerable Chao Kung;
The self-appointed Abbot of Shanghai,
After returning from yet one more far-flung

Soul-fishing expedition with disci-
Ples (thirteen, to be precise, believe it or not)
Who found themselves soon dominated by

This strangely charismatic polyglot
Angry tyrannical delusionist,
Who sucked them dry, and blew his stack, a lot;

An unabashed early apologist
For Japanese hegemony, who pleaded
That subjugation to an imperialist

TO TREBITSCH LINCOLN IN HELL

Superior race was just what China needed;
An advocate of world peace, whose demand
All governments resign, now, went unheeded;

The incubator of one final grand
Weird fantasy of global domination,
Whose overtures to Nazi High Command

With plans to start your own broadcasting station
For German propaganda in Tibet
Included offering a demonstration,

Once granted the requested tête-à-tête,
Your powers were vast and supernatural,
Claiming the moment you and Hitler met

Three wise men would emerge out of the wall
(This epochal entente was not to be);
A corpse at Shanghai General Hospital

On 6 October 1943.
How in the world did you pull all this off?
You must have had some disarming quality

To squirm your way to new trough after trough,
Some charm, some dazzle, plus tenacity:
Your enemies could fret and swear and scoff

At your inveterate ubiquity
But you would show them they weren't done with you,
Or you with them. Some bipolarity

Seems more than likely, for you cycled through
Your visionary highs and blacked-out lows
(Those lies were lies, but you believed them, too)

TO TREBITSCH LINCOLN IN HELL

As you aspired then plummeted then rose
In brilliant self-esteem then crashed and burned.
When your bizarre career drew to its close,

When oblivion faded and consciousness returned
And you found you were just another shade,
What dismal form of misery had you earned

With all the fuss you'd caused and mess you'd made?
When hideous Minos wrapped his horrid tail
Around himself, what devastating grade

Did he assign *your* life beyond the pale,
Assessing peccancy in bad events
Comprising your long compromising tale?

Not to the Circles of Incontinence,
Though you were qualified to share the pain,
With mistresses on several continents,

Of spirits buffeted by the hurricane
That drives and pounds the Lustful; or to lie
Helpless beneath the freezing, filthy rain

That soaks the howling Gluttons; or to cry
Along with the Avaricious and Prodigal
Circling in fruitless labor, as they try

To push huge weights with just their chests, and all
Collide together with a wrenching thud,
Turn, and slog back to stalemate; or to brawl

Among the Wrathful, coated in the crud
Of the River Styx; or, with the Sullen, sprawl
Face-downward, gurgling in its stinking mud.

TO TREBITSCH LINCOLN IN HELL

Not to the plain inside the buttressed wall
Of Dis, where, baked in flaming sepulchers,
The Heretics forever writhe and call

Out in convulsions, or where the Squanderers
Scramble in panic through the dreary wood
To stumble, caught and rent by packs of curs,

Though as a penal candidate you could
Fall either place, roasting or ripped to bits,
Were you not bound for a worse neighborhood.

Not even the steeply terraced torture pits
Of Malebolge would suit your foulest crime,
Though several of them wouldn't be bad fits,

Since Fraudulence you worked at, and full-time:
The First, where hornèd demons with long scourges
Lash the Seducers; the Seventh, where the slime

Of snakes joins that of Thieves, and what emerges
Is both and neither, a swallowing embrace
That fuses, morphs, and splits, then reconverges

As man and devouring serpent interlace
To slither from different creatures to the same,
Four limbs, two heads, one tail, one trunk, one face;

The Eighth, where clothed in all-consuming flame
The Fraudulent Counselors turn incinerated;
The Ninth, where in excruciating shame

The Sowers of Scandal and Schism get mutilated
In endless cycles, healing while reeling back
To suffer the sword of the demon designated

TO TREBITSCH LINCOLN IN HELL

To slash them back asunder with a hack,
Lopping a limb off here, a head off there,
Carving another open from mouth to crack;

The Tenth, the lowest and most awful, where,
Bloated and dropsical, the Falsifiers
Rot, wailing in the putrefying air,

Impersonators, Counterfeiters, Liars
All swollen, warped, tumescent. No, the dark
Logic of Dantesque punishment requires

Your classification by your blackest mark.
You must go all the way down, where Hell craters
Into the bitter, bone-chilling, and stark

Gelid extremes that freeze the wretched Traitors,
To Antenora, from whose glacial lake
The heads of those infernal calculators

Who turn against their homeland jut and quake,
Chattering in unending agony,
Or, miserable, to motionlessly ache

In terminal Judecca, where you'd be
Fastened, encased from head to toe in ice
Like a wisp of straw in glass, for treachery

To benefactors. There you would pay the price
For crimes that didn't, were retribution so
Ordered and allegorically precise.

Would your crimes were the worst we came to know.

✣

SKY BURIAL

Wherever the soul goes,
On top of the world the body is broken and eaten.
For three ceremonial days
It is washed in scented water, tended
By monks, while the soul stays,
Roaming the body, confused (on what threshold who knows?),
Bereft and grieving,
And, as it lingers, is read to
From *The Tibetan Book of the Dead*, to
Soften and sweeten
Its trauma, and guide its leaving.
Then, all that ended,

The soul having departed,
They crumple the empty body, snapping its back
To fold it up quite small,
And take it, on a palanquin,
To the sky burial
Plateau, where, with an art that seems cold-hearted
To other cultures,
Gutted, flesh chopped bite-sized,
Skull and brains smashed, bones pulverized
And mixed with yak
Butter, it's fed to the vultures
Now crowding in,

Summoned, for centuries,
By windings of the sky-horn, and a fire
Of juniper twigs, to eat
The mortal parts of everyone,
Our organs, gristle, meat.
These emanations of white *dakinis*
Assimilate
And raise us, even dying
In upper atmosphere, as, flying
Ever higher,
They disarticulate
In wind and sun.

HEARING VOICES

Whose voice is this, just audible through static?
Crinkled and interrupted, to be sure,
But, even though the medium's impure,
Hypnotic, orotund, and automatic,

The grumbling baritone of Tennyson
Reciting, again, "The Charge of the Light Brigade"
As wave on wave the syllables crest and fade:
"*Some* one had *blun*der'd," as they'd often done.

And whose is this? Pitched in a higher key,
The almost Bostonian, tartly nasal "a"
Accenting what the good man had to say
To fellow citizens, robustly free,

Speaking in words, no chanting metronome
Of golden phrases from the treasure vault,
But idiosyncratic Uncle Walt
Just talking to us, smiling and at home

In his "America." The primitive
Technology that Edison invented
Captured articulations represented
As paraffin and beeswax let them live,

Echoing down to ears in distant ages
(Like hopeful capsules launched far into space
To signal someone we're the human race)
The voices fallen silent on their pages.

KING LEAR

Of course some wise guy *would* nickname him "King,"
That Princeton rookie with his college ring
Pitching for Cincinnati, who finished last.
He couldn't hit, or run, or throw it fast,
And didn't binge or brawl or anything,
Just floated a knuckleball they swung right past.

A player's tale: the spotlight of renown
Switched off, you're yesterday's ticket, out of town
And back to Charles. He hurt his arm next year
And he was gone like luck, or penny beer.
And when an old man's mourners set him down
In wind and rain, who knew he was King Lear?

✣

HAMLET

It's quiet here. A stoic rectitude
Props up the weather-pummeled citizens,
Craggy yet almost cheerful. Uniform
Gray granite cottages, precipitous
And sturdy, make the most of things. The wind
Does all the talking hereabouts, and who
Would think to think about the universe?
Their certainties define them, not their doubts.

✣

ICE AGE ART

Fashioned by firelight, nicked and scooped and planed
By crude flint burins nibbed to scrape and hone
Till something like a miracle remained
On bone and antler, ivory and stone,

Where hours of pinpoint labor left behind,
Faithful to details of anatomy,
First inklings of the panoramic mind
In polished, miniature menagerie,

The animals that peopled their stark scene
Of snow drift, barren, glacial watercourse
(Bison, musk ox, mammoth, wolverine,
Cave bear, cave lion, reindeer, ibex, horse)

Hardened to artifact in action poses
(Galloping, swimming, leaping onto prey):
Paleolithic artwork presupposes,
For subsequent endeavors to this day,

Compulsions to creation that inform
Signs of the origin—there at the start
To mine the world to mime the world, and form
The ur-fidelities of Ice Age art.

FIDELITIES

Whatever piece of code,
Hard-wired millennia, dictates they cross
    The Himalayan chain
To reach their distant wintertime abode,
    Reliving all the strain
Of their monumental journey's struggle and loss,
    The graceful Demoiselle Crane,

    Anthropoides virgo,
Slender and beautiful, known by its white
    Ear tufts and long black breast
Plume, seems too frail to, year after driven year, go
    On such an arduous quest,
Scaling those glacial summits in its flight,
    Then crossing back to nest

    In marshes on the steppes,
Where their peculiar courtship rituals
    Require elaborate
Wing-flaps, and bows, and odd, balletic steps,
    As they communicate
In long duets, coordinating calls
    To single out a mate

    For life. Fidelity
So perfect moved Valmiki (so goes the tale)
    By the Tamasa Stream,
Who saw a loving couple suddenly
    Divide like a ripped seam
Split when a hunter's arrow felled the male,
    And heard the female scream

FIDELITIES

In her bewildered grief,
And felt his anger surge spontaneously
    To sharpen to a curse
Wishing the killer unrest without relief:
    The world's first man-made verse,
In a form of metrical dexterity
    Whole epics would rehearse.

    Metapoetic birds,
The *Koonj* (from *kraunch*, like "crane") can represent
    Feminine loveliness
In delicately curved dimensions words
    Take figures to finesse,
Or those whose wanderings of long extent
    Their journeyings express

    Through parallel's conceit,
For what exhausted traveler, far from home,
    Looking for one small source
Of strength or hope, would not admire their feat
    Of pluck and subtle force,
Braving the altitudes to overcome
    The hazards of the course?

    (Fatigue, hunger, predation
Defeat the laboring heart's heroic rallies
    Every difficult day:
In the length of each biannual migration
    Thousands will drop away.)
We know now that they don't cut through the valleys,
    But somehow fight their way

FIDELITIES

    Right up to clear the top
Of ridges as high as 26,000 feet,
    Riding the thermals so
They elevate (it's death to start to stop)
    Above sheer ice and snow
To hit, head on, the big winds, beat and beat
    Against the blast, then go

    Over at last to glide
Downward on resting wings, till some prenatal
    Instinct decides it's time
To turn their faces toward the great divide
    And, in formation, climb
To meet the wind-tormented, often fatal
    Precincts of the sublime.

HARRISON'S CLOCK

Even the most recalcitrant conundrum,
Most enigmatic brain-teaser, most baffling,
    Perplexedly stupefying
  And dilemmatic quandary,
    Logic-defying,
Which brings our rut-inhabiting and humdrum
    Intelligence to some
  Impenetrable boundary,
Some blind spot, some unfathomable sum
    And sets us waffling,
  Imprisoned by polarities
(Nature or nurture? particle or wave?),
    Some cul-de-sac or cave
  Murky with deep obscurities

—Dark energy, dark matter, neutrino mass,
Cantor's infinities, Schrödinger's cat,
    The source of gamma rays,
  The seven bridges of Königsberg,
    The intricate "maze
Of moral relativism" (or turf, or grass,
    Or maize), a better mousetrap,
  The IT nightmare of Rube Goldberg
Data base management, an honest house trap
    Repair, a fat-
Free diet that satisfies, the sins
Of fathers visiting yet one more time,
    The perfect, victimless crime,
    The origin of origins—

HARRISON'S CLOCK

Yields sometimes, in the end, not to the flights
Of fancy speculation, sidereal charts,
    Or the pure good of theory,
  But to the dull, mechanical,
      Patient and weary
Labors of tedious days and troubled nights
    Through trials that fail and fail,
  Obsession's grim, tyrannical
Absorption in the pickiest detail,
    The stubborn arts
Of the compulsive, focused will,
Accepting the perfectionist's confinement
    In quest of what refinement
  Can amplify her growing skill:

For instance, the holy grail of navigation,
Discovering one's longitude at sea,
    Which vexed such intellects
    As Newton, Halley, Euler, Hooke,
      And caused the wrecks
Of countless ships (one horrid illustration:
    Their reckoning off by miles
  Despite procedures by the book,
Two thousand sailors died on the Scilly Isles,
    A tragedy
  That spurred the fabled Longitude Act,
Establishing a monetary prize
    Of unprecedented size
  For any reasonably exact

HARRISON'S CLOCK

Solution), was found not by ephemerides
Like Galileo's, or Flamsteed's catalog
    Mapping celestial motion,
  Or any correction for the flux
    Of trackless ocean
Using the stars and moon as luminous guides,
    Or more unlikely helps
  Proposed to resolve the fiendish crux,
Like timing the pathetic howls and yelps
    Of a tortured dog
  Using "powder of sympathy,"
Or stationing ships with guns to fire away
    Appointed times of day
  At intervals across the sea,

But a self-taught provincial, an abrupt,
Obscure clock-maker, one John Harrison,
    Whose artistry reformed
  The craft of the chronometric trade,
    As he transformed
The laggard clock, forever interrupt-
    Ed by wear and winding, fall-
  Ing out of time, to a home-made
Baroque high-tech device precise past all
    Comparison,
  Equipped to counteract the raw
Conditions (changes in humidity,
    Temperature, gravity,
  And barometric pressure, the yaw

HARRISON'S CLOCK

And pitch of shipboard, the insidious
Corrosion of salt air, each variable
    Conducive to mistakes)
By carpentry, taking in hand
      Clamps, scrapers, stakes,
Tongs, saws, screw arbors with fastidious
    Mastery, calibrated
By innovation on demand
Of all the staggering gadgets he created,
    Very able
To rig up what he needed—pairing
Brass and steel in the bi-metallic strip,
    Countering friction's grip
    By inventing the ball bearing,

Plus other gifts he found just feeling his way,
The gridiron pendulum, the grasshopper
    Escapement, lubrication
    Via lignum vitae—to mechanize
      Close calculation
In his great sea clocks' brilliant brass display
    Of balance and precision,
    Of whirring wheels that harmonize
With rods and springs and dials in timely vision,
    Each show-stopper
Proving, as Hogarth said, "one of
The most exquisite movements ever made,"
    A spectacular cascade
    Unwinding long labors of love

HARRISON'S CLOCK

(Love of the object, true—true love of art,
Of tiny fillips no one else will see,
    Of ornamental function
  Fusing resistant elements
      In taut conjunction
Of form with force and shimmering part with part),
  "H1," the toast of all
  London, "H2," which represents
Breakthrough minute adjustments, most of all
    "Harrison 3,"
  The master's "curious third machine,"
An odd assembly of balances and gears
    That cost him nineteen years
  To streamline, till, lighter and lean,

Comprising seven hundred and fifty-three
Separate parts, it too sat in its box,
    Polished and perfected
  Only, just like the other two,
    To be rejected
By its creator, and never go to sea,
    When Harrison decided
  A fantastic pocket watch would do,
If built along the principles that guided
    The three sea clocks,
  Even better once put to the test
By the Board of Longitude's adjudication
    Of Parliament's stipulation
  For success, a voyage to the West

HARRISON'S CLOCK

Indies, on which the watch, "Harrison 4,"
Its miniaturized machinery
    Sheer jewel, ruby pins
    And diamond pallets cut so fine
        The tiny ins
And outs of wheel and lever have all the more
    Capacity to amaze,
    Performed superbly right down the line,
Losing a mere five seconds in eighty-one days,
    Though chicanery
    Orchestrated by wily Nevil
Maskelyne, a biased, contrarian,
    Committed Lunarian
    Who was Harrison's personal devil,

Succeeded in denying him the Prize
On a bureaucratic technicality
    (Royal intervention
    Was necessary to reward
        The man's invention
And, after trial and torment, recognize
    That the watch could, in fact,
    Although the Board was not on board,
Within the clear requirements of the Act
    Keep time at sea),
    While all three clocks got commandeered
By Maskelyne, in order to be "tested,"
    Suddenly, rudely wrested
    From a man he both despised and feared

HARRISON'S CLOCK

To be trundled over cobbles, disrespected,
Manhandled, dropped, and ultimately ruled
    Failures, then locked away
  By their peevish, petty enemy,
      To rust and decay
In a damp closet, dirty, unwound, neglected,
    Dismissed by jealous slander,
  To wait for more than a century
Until the labors of Lieutenant Commander
      Rupert T. Gould
  (Who toiled, unpaid, a dozen years
On painstaking and meticulous restoration,
    In service to the nation,
    Of mainspring barrels, winding gears,

And steel check-pieces on the balance springs)
Would reconstruct their works and set them right
      And running, to this day,
  In Flamsteed House, where, venerated,
      On bright array,
They are marveled at as timeless, beautiful things,
    Even "H3," which seems
  To stand ("not merely complicated,
It is abstruse") for art that risks extremes
      To keep, despite
  Each disappointment and hard knock,
Despite the machinations of rival schools
    And telling deafness of fools,
      Pitch perfect time, like Harrison's clock.

SHAKESPEARE'S HORSE

He was a man knew horses, so we moved
As wills were one, and all was won at will,
In hand with such sleight handling as improved
Those parks and parcels where we're racing still,

Pounding like pairs of hooves or pairs of hearts
Through woodland scenes and lush, dramatic spaces,
With all our parts in play to play all parts
In pace with pace to put us through his paces.

Ages have passed. All channels channel what
Imagined these green plots and gave them names
Down to the smallest role, if and and but,
What flies the time (the globe gone up in flames),

What thunders back to ring the ringing course
And runs like the streaking will, like Shakespeare's horse.

SOMETIMES I DREAM
THAT I AM NOT
WALT WHITMAN

Once, when he was a very old man, he came across a notebook he had kept as a boy, in which he had copied out poems by poets he particularly admired—Blake, Kipling, the early Yeats. His memory had now deteriorated to the point where he no longer recognized what these were, but mistook them for his own youthful compositions. He found himself in tears, surprised and delighted to discover, in his long forgotten juvenilia, such confidence, such skill, and such originality ...

— J. H. Hobson, *A Human Touch: The Poetry of William Karl*

RIVER OF SONG

Who *said* that?
           Surfacing from sleep,
Seeing the curtains fringed with light,
I hear a music fading. Whose?
Part mine, part someone's. Cold and deep
The word-flow runs, and dark as night.

The dead keep singing. They don't sleep.
We wake, diminishing, and write.
I hear a music playing. Whose?
On runs the river, dark and deep
And cold as interstellar night.

I.

DERECHO

We didn't know the word, until it raced
Into the headlines, swamped the blogosphere,
    Shot tweets and postings, lightning-paced,
        From devastated scenes,
        And scrolled across our screens
    With "WARNING/FLASH FLOODS/STORMS/SEVERE"

As fast as when dark shelves of cloud arrive
Riding the gust front of a straight-line storm
    Huge downburst clusters swell and dive
        Unleashing hurricane-
        Force blasts of wind and rain,
    A squall line in bow echo form

With supercells and bookend vortices
Barrels for hours across hundreds of miles,
    Flips cars, flips trailers, jerks up trees,
        Peels roofs and levels walls,
        Grounds power poles and scrawls
    Its signature in rubbish piles

And strewn detritus all along its path
Of instantaneous destruction, cause
    To see some deity's hurled wrath
        In black skies and black rain,
        Some monster pleased by pain
    Batting our poor lives with its paws

Or pouncing down to rip the world askew
With one sharp thundrous cataclysmic blow,
    Crashing the lexicon. Right through.
        Wind-battered, water-blurred,
        We didn't know this word
    For "ruinous." But now we know.

STOPPING

Whose woods these are we all know well
Though, tight-lipped, most refuse to tell,
Reluctant to assume the cost
Of any silly, childish spell

To make such hidden things stay lost:
No wind no ice no snow no frost,
No solid winter six feet deep
Nor'easter-swirled and bluster-tossed

Now blanketing a world asleep
Beneath the dark sky's starless sweep,
None of that. Just my double-take
To find, at my age, I still keep

Making my typical mistake,
Stopping beside this frozen lake
When I have promises to break
And miles to go before I wake.

ECHOLOCATION

Just as the bottlenose or pipistrelle
    Can map the world by sound
  With clicks and squeaks and high-pitched pings
    Emitted to rebound
    Through ocean or night air,
    Enabling them to tell
      Precisely where
    Tasty or nasty things
    Might swarm or swim or lurk
In thick dark or in liquid murk,
Using cochlear adaptation
    As fine-tuned instrument
For foraging and navigation
    In lieu of sight or scent,

So this tries, as it sings both high and low,
    Flicking in fricatives
And whispering in sibilants,
    To bounce back off what gives
    A rising assonance
    To every rounded "o,"
      A resonance
    Echoing those first chants
    Projecting songs to come
In fine-tuning the medium
To double, treble, crest, and flow
    With "sun," " moon," "morning star,"
Like flocks of leaves, by which we know
    Exactly where we are.

OROGENESIS

When moonstruck spirits said
To William Butler Yeats,
"We've come to give you metaphors
For poetry," this isn't what they meant:
An upward buckling of tectonic plates
That elevated ocean floors,
One hell-raising Devonian event
Whose record can be read

In long striated strips
Of orogenic belts,
In seashells found on mountaintops
And smooth granitic batholiths. On shifts
Of molten tides the crust thickens or melts,
The viscous circle never stops,
The roaring river spits and splits and lifts,
The mantle, sliding, slips

So quakes and tremors scar
Our psyches and our lands,
For any pretty hillside town
Built near a jagged fault, even with care
And solid stuff, by practiced, steady hands,
Can in a flash come crashing down
As tragic cries inflect the dust-filled air
And landscape stands ajar.

Nothing is stable, static.
Surface is always flow.
Structures of posed placidity,
The chiseled symmetries of form, conceal
Compressed volcanic agony below,
Intemperate liquidity
Whose outbursts, unpredictable, reveal
A flare for the dramatic

OROGENESIS

      Ambition to ascend.
     Thrust by deforming thrust
    The fresh material extrudes,
And year by year the Himalayas rise,
Mounting colliding continental crust
    At clear breath-taking altitudes
To redefine the precinct of the skies
      From which the clouds depend.

     Not even mountains last
      Forever, but when all
Is said they last a good long time.
"Not marble nor the gilded monuments"
Sustain comparison with what we'll call
    The geological sublime,
Or what is, gauged by proper instruments,
      New, and coming up fast.

AUTOPOIESIS

Some truths it might be shrewder *not* to tell.
Take the example of the single cell,
Eukaryotic, compartmentalized,
From man, or plant, or mold, however sized,
With membrane, nucleus, and organelles.
The self-maintaining chemistry of cells
Renders a thing intact, autonomous,
Whether alone, or deep inside of us,
So organized that every transformation
Becomes another act of self-creation,
A unity of network, a machine
That allocates each acid and protein
Its proper role and place inside the whole
That is itself its proper place and role.
As Maturana and Varela saw,
The neat dynamic of this inner law
Offers a polymorphous metaphor
Adaptable to what we want it for,
To systems theory, sociology,
Or literary studies. Poetry
Accommodates such figuring of what
Is not unlike a couplet snapping shut,
Leaving us outside. What we set in play
Insists on having its peculiar say
To spin the world it shapes, inscribed, compact,
The heartless, self-affirming artifact
Whose firework canopy and diamond show
Tell us the truth lies where we'd best not go.
Marking the interface of sound and sense,
The poem is its own intelligence
Out there alone and making making do.
It doesn't need me, reader, or need you.

THE DEMON DINANUKHT

Sunk in his chair, he seems half man, half book,
Inhabiting both worlds, reading himself
To sleep beside his drink, though he may lie
About falling asleep, half man half book,
And even lie about reading, himself.

And you have felt, yourself, half man, half book,
Felt someone else entirely, reading himself
Right through you, past you, riffs of sea and sky
Turning the ruffled page, half man half book
Drifting between blue worlds, reading himself.

The demon Dinanukht, half man, half book,
Idles between the worlds, reading himself.
Lifetimes he turns his pages, seated by
The waters clear as glass, half man half book
Perfecting his reflection, reading himself.

And Old John Wallace seemed half man half book
Turning to winter air, reading himself
Accumulating in slow drifts of sky,
Old man, old massive head, half man, half book,
Half dying star, half starlight, reading himself.

MARK STRAND

When I came to the end of the dream, there was Mark Strand.
We were in a vast hall, where the ceiling was too high to see,
And the light slanted down from above, and a cold wind blew.
We sat on a bench in the back. A little ways off,
A teacher was teaching a class, and she asked him to speak,
But he shook his head: he was too tired. Then he turned
To me, and he said, "I don't write anymore. I don't
Even look at the moon. But I read." Then he smiled. "When you read
The books you most love for the last time, you see
The great works of imagination get better and better.
When you come to that passage where, arrayed in battalions,
With all their flashing armor and flapping banners
And bright wings fanning the starlight, the heavenly host
Throws down its spears, you wonder, although you've read it
A hundred times, 'Will it really happen again?,'
And when it does, you are surprised." There were tears
In his eyes as he said this. But were they tears of sadness,
Or tears of joy, or were they just caused by the wind,
That cold wind blowing and blowing? Then he was gone,
And the teacher was gone, with her class, and the students' voices,
And all I could hear in the hall was the sound of the wind.

THE END WAS OVER

The end was over, over long ago.
If others survived in isolated places
Beyond the horizon, we had no way to know.

No one remembered names, or styles, or faces.
Perhaps some thoughts occurred, but no one spoke.
If travelers passed by, they left no traces.

Were someone to tell a story or a joke
No one would even begin to understand.
If someone walked out on the ice, it broke.

Things happened or didn't happen. Nothing was planned.
We moved more slowly when we tried to hurry.
It hindered us if someone lent a hand.

What little we could see was always blurry.
All we could hear was silence everywhere.
Perhaps we should have worried. We didn't worry.

Perhaps we should have cared. We didn't care
Enough to leave those will-numbing confines,
All vacancy and stillness and cold air,

Where signs meant nothing. Not that there were signs.
There was no central point from which to see
The emptiness keep forming empty lines

That led us back to us. And who were "we"?
There was no "we" left. Everyone was gone.
The only person left was only me.

In that white world I was myself alone
The figure of a man against the snow.
The wind droned on, unending, monotone.

I liked it there. But that was long ago.

ELEGY FOR THE AMERICAN SUBLIME

And what, in the end, can the solitary man
Make of the landscape he's projected by?
A few dead leaves, the puny, denuded trees,
The emptiness filling up with nothing at all?

The annals of the American sublime
Shrink to a handful of names, then forget the names.
The sun comes up on a terrified new world
Stripped of its rich, protective coverings,

Its canopies, its finial adjectives,
Its columned boreal abundancies,
Its tropical imbrications of this and that.
The ice shelves crack and calve into the seas.

Across the wide waste a solitary bird
Flies straight through the center of absence, then flies on.
The thought of a palm tree never crosses its mind.
It navigates mnemonic indices

Although the world it remembers no longer exists,
The wetlands no longer exist, Key West is long gone.
If it lands, it will imagine an audience
Imagining a song. Then it will sing.

II.

SOMETIMES I DREAM THAT I AM NOT WALT WHITMAN

Sometimes I dream that I am not Walt Whitman,
That I am an engineer, or an airplane pilot,
Or a schoolteacher, or a soldier, or a traveling salesman,
Not a poet living his afterlife through his poems.

I enjoy those dreams. I enjoy waking to find they were only dreams.

LET THEM SAY WHATEVER THEY WANT

Let them say whatever they want about me on the Internet,
I am fine with it. I am all for communication in an instant.

I like the Internet, but sometimes it makes me feel like an old man.
Then I remember: I am only one hundred and ninety-nine.

RETURNING TO THE SEA-SHORE

Returning to the sea-shore after more than a century
I dally my feet in the waves as I did when a boy,
I see the developments, the condominia, then I do not see them at all,
Just the marsh grass and the cattails covering the dunes,
The long, low clouds and the dark rolling shroud of the sea.

I HEAR IT IS CHARGED AGAINST ME

I hear it is charged against me that I have become an institution,
A monument, a study, an industry,
With biographers and bibliographers and editorial apparatuses.

In my lifetime I didn't much care about institutions,
And now in my afterlife I care even less.
Whatever they say I am, you can be certain I'm not.

Please desist with your commentaries and annotations, however well intended,
For they are completely beside the point, and always will be.
Go walk in the fields and woods, go walk by the sea at night and look up at the stars.

See what I mean? Yes, now you see what I mean.

LIKE A GHOST I RETURNED

Like a ghost I returned to my old house in Camden
And tagged along with a tour group, listening to the guide
Recite details of my life there, some of them true.

I saw, one more time, the room where I slept and wrote
(They had my old pen on display, I could almost reach out and
    touch it),
The room where I sat with guests, the kitchen where Mary cooked
    for me,
The room where they laid out my corpse and a thousand people
    filed past.

Who would have thought I had so many friends and admirers?
And what did they think they would see? It was just a corpse.
The real me had moved on, living and breathing in poems.

I am no staid collection of facts and artifacts.

I am the waves in the seas of grass, I am the wind in the leaves.

SOME TUESDAYS I GO TO LISBON

Some Tuesdays I go to Lisbon to see my friend Álvaro de Campos.
We walk down to the docks and watch the boats come in,
Or stroll up the Rua do Ouro, or visit his favorite tobacco shop,
All the time talking about what's real and what isn't.

He imagines I have serenity, and envies me for it.
But I am not serene, even now that I'm posthumous,
And I certainly wasn't serene when I had a body,
Just accepting of everything.

I try to explain the difference, but he can't quite hear it.

He thinks he is nothing (he isn't), and savors his misery, his boredom.
I suspect it depresses him that he was never a person,
That he only lived in poems, and in peoples' minds,
But I only live in poems, and in peoples' minds,
So there is less difference between us than there would be if he
    were human.

I guess it cheers him up when I point this out, but I can't really tell.
One minute he's moping, the next minute he's running in circles,
    shouting ecstatically.

He always asks me to stay a few days, or a week.
But on Wednesdays I go to Chile, to see Pablo Neruda.

MY OLD CAMERADO, MY BODY

My old camerado, my body, how long has it been?

You from whom I was indivisible, to whom I adhered,
One with me, one with the best of me, the best part of me, all of me,
You whose sensations would dazzle and overwhelm me
Until all my thoughts were electric and nothing but,
Diminished, over the years, to a slight tingling,
Then to only the ghost of a tingling,
The memory of a memory of a memory.

Today I'm not sure I would recognize my own face.

There is, I admit, a peace of sorts in cessation,
A release from desire, from desire's waiting and hoping.
I suppose I should be grateful, but I don't feel grateful.
I am the poet of the body who has no body.
Nobody tallies that loss more surely than I do
As I sing one last song for you, my old camerado, my body.

III.

RUNAWAY BLIMP

     On daily walks I'd seen
      It shimmer in the eastern sky,
Glossed with an eerily synthetic sheen
Early morning light would intensify,
Afloat like an air-borne precipitate
Hanging, ethereal and argentine,
    By its bright, identical mate
       High above Aberdeen,

     On trial, when inflated
    And raised, as JLENS, or Joint Land
Attack Cruise Missile Defense Elevated
Netted Sensor System, part of a planned
Upgrade of East Coast aerial surveillance
Whose virtues, prematurely celebrated
    For scope, precision, instant valence,
      Proved much exaggerated:

     The blimp struggled to track
    Objects in flight, discriminate
Our friendly stuff from stuff that might attack,
Or quickly, properly communicate
With all the crisscrossed elements of air
Defense, bumping its "activation" back
    For yet more tweaking and repair,
      Drawing Congressional flak

     As costs ballooned, and it
    Was tagged a "zombie program," loss
Piled high on loss (deterring not a whit
Its advocate, General James E. "Hoss"
Cartwright, who fought to keep it, then signed on
After retirement, as lax rules permit,
    To serve its maker, Raytheon,
      For handsome benefit),

RUNAWAY BLIMP

Symbolic of the bloated
Unindustrious complex, bought
And sold, the useless, shamelessly promoted
Gadgets unneeded in the wars unfought,
As representatives who know the score
Protect the massive boondoggles they floated
    And, past the fast revolving door,
        Get paid for how they voted;

    And now, as if to make
    A show of excess run amok
And prove its project one big fat mistake,
A multi-billion dollar clusterfuck,
Taking advantage of some windy weather
The blimp has wriggled loose and made a break,
    Dragging its mile-long Kevlar tether
        In its destructive wake,

        Sans clue or caveat,
    For random parts unknown, gone rogue
While flummoxed handlers wonder where it's at,
Turned star, meme-of-the-moment, Twitter vogue,
When scattered residents happen to spy
("O Amos, gookamoedoe!" "What is *that*?"),
    Lurching across the autumn sky,
        The errant aerostat

    Which can't self-disenable
    (The fail-safe mechanism failed
Once the unstable ship got too unstable)
To stop percussive impacts now entailed
As side effects of blimpomania,
As right through power line and fence and stable
    For swaths of Pennsylvania
        Swings of its massive cable

RUNAWAY BLIMP

    Slice arbitrarily,
  Careening off like pumped-up teens
On a joyride, intoxicated, free,
Though now tracked by two scrambled F-16s,
And when state troopers, sent to do it in
Once it descends and gets snagged on a tree,
    Pepper its self-repairing skin
        With shotguns, finally

    It shrivels back to land,
  Downed in Moreland Township, PA,
And soon they'll want to know at High Command
Why some fool things just up and run away,
Like love, or metaphor, or public debt, so
Bigwigs and pointy-heads might understand
    How such a costly craft could get so
        Completely out of hand.

SONG OF THE NRA

"Guns don't kill people, people do,"
People with guns. Our native right
To stroll forth armed for mortal fight
Will stand its ground. It might kill you,
It might kill me, or anyone.
America I've got my gun!

A firearm doesn't pull the trigger
Each time a toddler shoots a parent.
We need more rifles, that's apparent,
Sleek, rapid-fire, and better, bigger.
There's one that's right for everyone.
America I've got my gun!

In bars, in churches, parks and schools
We'd best be armed. If they attack
We'll whip our guns out and fight back.
We'll shoot it out like bloody fools
While people scream and duck and run.
America I've got my gun!

Murder might as well be mass.
Register the numbers slain
At a movie, on a train,
Little children in a class,
People dancing, having fun ...
America I've got my gun!

Orlando, Blacksburg, Columbine,
Newtown, Charleston, San Ysidro,
Aurora, and San Bernardino ...
But Congress better toe the line
Or someone to their right will run.
Just watch yourself. I've got my gun.

EASTER 2016

Hatred and fear surge on the bitter winds.
New ignorance gives credence to each lie,
The demagogue echoes the roiling cry.
Our common sense of purpose, whipsawed, bends
And starts to splinter. Urged by the angry storm,
Worst things worsen. The body politic
Gnaws its own innards, retches, grows more sick.
The harmed are drawn to what would do more harm.

Target the other, blame it all on Them
And down we go, shot by the messenger.
Such ugly means mean even uglier ends
Would body-slam the hapless passenger.
Hatred and fear surge on the bitter winds.
Dark hour. Rough beast. The slouch towards Bethlehem.

THE RETREAT

after Hugo

It snowed. Now, self-defeated by conquest,
For the first time the eagle had failed a test.
Dark days! Slowly the emperor returned.
Behind his back, Moscow still smoked and burned.
It snowed. From winter's avalanche of pain
After each white plain rose another white plain.
One couldn't make out companies or flags.
A great army turned a herd of scraps and rags.
No one could tell the center from the flanks.
It snowed. The wounded sheltered against the flanks
Of frozen horses; sentinels were ghosts;
The silent buglers, frigid at their posts,
Sat rigid in their saddles, dusted with snow,
Lips fastened to the horns they could not blow.
Grape-shot and musket-balls, mixed with snow-flakes,
Kept raining; shivering, pondering mistakes,
Grenadiers wandered, mustaches caked with ice.
It snowed, it always snowed. Wind gripped like a vice.
Soldiers, marching, slipped on ground glazed with frost,
Stumbling, barefoot and starving, utterly lost.
The men of war, no heart left to fight back,
Shadows against the dark sky, black on black,
Filed through the mist like dreams of misery.
Pure solitude, huge, horrible to see,
Surrounded them in silent retribution.
The snow kept up its quiet contribution,
A great white shroud blanketing the whole force.
The doomed knew they would die, alone of course.
How to escape the country's double curse?
Two foes: the tsar, the north. The north was worse.
They scrapped the cannons; the carriages were used
For firewood. Those who lay down died. Confused,
Dejected, they kept retreating. The white waste
Consumed them. One whole regiment was erased
While sleeping, buried by folds of snow, undone
As pulverized by Hannibal or the Hun.
Wagons and stretchers, the wounded, the half-dead

THE RETREAT

Jammed bridges, crushed together as they fled.
Ten thousand fell asleep, one hundred woke.
Ney, who once moved an army when he spoke,
Squabbled over his watch with three Cossacks.
Each night the alarm would sound. Then the attacks.
The spectral soldiers grabbed their guns, surrounded
By a rushing, terrifying blur that sounded
Like shrieking vultures, circling, striking again,
Appalling squadrons, whirlwinds of wild men.
An army was destroyed in one dark night.
Still the emperor lingered, watching their flight,
As a giant oak tree, subject to the axe
When calamity, the cutter, scales and attacks
Its grandeur, though still standing and still tall,
Shudders watching its lopped-off branches fall.
Commanders and soldiers died, each in their turn.
A remaining few believers could discern,
Huddling in devotion around his tent,
How his shadow on the canvas came and went.
Not knowing what to think, quailed, stupefied,
The emperor turned to God; his glorious pride
Trembled. Seeing his legions scattered about
Dead and dying, Napoleon cried out
(Presuming the destined settling of some score),
"Is this my punishment, great God of War?"
And then he heard, out of the shadows and snow,
A voice pronounce his name, and answer: "No."

COULROPHOBIA WITH LINE FROM AUDEN

Each day we're pummeled by the news.
The morning's storm of nasty tweets
Gathers a pool of exegetes.
The President's in golfing shoes.

Whipped commentators commentate
Upon a world flipped upside down.
Sad props to our commanding clown
Collapse in a reeling crisis state

Out of control he isn't in.
Tools the lobbies brought and sold
Open a fake news Age of Gold.
The public takes it, on the chin.

Meanwhile more vulnerable, vast
Networks of ecosystem start
To melt and dry and break apart,
Silently and very fast.

IV.

PLEIN AIR

What *is* this landscape, rising like a dream
Through somnolent evasions of the mind?
A bay, some boats, a sand bar, a blue sky,
The bluest sky, clear water, aquamarine,
Two green peninsular hills to frame the scene,
The boats becalmed or anchored, and, far out,
A steamer stuck all silent afternoon,
The only agitation dips and swerves
Of frigate birds and pelicans and gulls ...

It might be Martinique, or Guadeloupe,
Or Dominica, or some other isle.
It might be paradise, it might be real—
The world we dream on when we dream the world
Is picture perfect, and we're outside time
Or time has grown so large there is no time
Or all the time in the world to linger here
Where palm tree fronds apportion zones of shade,
To sip the essences of sea and sky
Like some exotic drink, and feel, just now,
The tiniest intentions of a breeze.

And we know it was never always this way
And ever will be, the two of us, alone
Together in the sunshot world blended
By memory, until the light declines
And all we loved to look on dims, obscured,
And sign by sign the alien stars arise.

THE EKPHRASTIC POET

The ekphrastic poet seeks a fine vignette
For the conjunction of the sister arts.
He looks and looks. He hasn't found it yet.

He wants a scene too vivid to forget,
A whole composed of quintessential parts
An ekphrastic poet needs for his vignette:

A still life, maybe, wineglass with baguette,
Or rustic view, with oxen pulling carts.
He looks, and looks. He hasn't found it, yet

Believes in it. He hardly feels regret
For all the botched approaches, the false starts.
The ekphrastic poet sees his first vignette

Will take more looking. Arranging his *palette*
In imitation of the color charts,
He looks as if he hasn't found it yet.

When the spectrum forms a secret alphabet,
When words turn pictures, or when spades turn hearts,
The ekphrastic poet seizes his vignette.
For now, he looks. He hasn't found it. Yet.

HARVEST HOBSON

He was a poet, but the poets who garnered praise
And paraded about admired by everyone
Were ones he despised (no wit, no irony,
Faux-philosophical pretentiousness),
And most of all he hated Harvest Hobson,
A poet who wasn't nearly as good as himself.

He decided to take the whole gang on himself,
Composing a panegyric of mock praise
In the form of a scathing essay on Harvest Hobson
For a publication read by everyone,
"Harvest Hobson and the New Pretentiousness,"
A wicked assault of withering irony.

But no one seemed to get the irony.
They came away believing he himself
Was a fan of what he called "Pretentiousness,"
Thought it a noble thing, deserving praise,
And that he really felt, like everyone,
Nothing but admiration for Harvest Hobson.

His essay helped secure, for Harvest Hobson,
A major prize. The bitterest irony
Was suddenly to be seen by everyone
As the champion of Hobson, who thanked him himself,
To be known, now, as a critic, and receive praise
As the bold advocate of Pretentiousness.

He authored a screed against Pretentiousness,
Viciously ridiculing Harvest Hobson
As a poet unworthy of notice, much less praise,
Without the slightest hint of irony.
From the moment it appeared, he found himself
Cursed, hated, and insulted by everyone,

HARVEST HOBSON

His talks and readings canceled, every one,
A snake whose treacherous pretentiousness
Had led him, desperate to promote himself,
To attack his benefactor, Harvest Hobson,
To whom he had once bent even his iron knee.
He grew confused, unable to appraise

A poem, or tell himself from Harvest Hobson.
They were one and the same. Perhaps pretentiousness
Was better than irony, and worthy of praise.

THE ALBATROSS

after Baudelaire

Often, to amuse themselves, the sailors seize
What shadows their ship as it glides along its way,
The albatross, high lord of the gulfs and seas,
Their indolent companion turned their prey.

Hobbled on shipboard, baffled, the sky king's
Deposed, a joke his dignity abhors.
Clumsy, ashamed, he feels his huge white wings
Drag at his sides, useless as unmanned oars.

This soaring voyager, how awkward and weak,
How comical, tormented by the crew!
One torturer sticks a cutty in his beak;
Limping, one mimics the cripple who once flew.

The poet, like this rider of the skies,
Wandered the trade winds, laughing at earth-bound things,
But grounded where people hoot and criticize
Can't walk, encumbered by his outsized wings.

GIOTTO IN PADUA

Arena Chapel

A blue so blue it seems the radiant day
Has entered the room without the glittering
Sunlight, so deep, so soft the flittering
Angels look real as birds as they loop away

Above these curves of rediscovered mass,
Delineated body taking form
Beneath those robes (ground: flatness was the norm),
Fresco by fresco, here. It came to pass:

Clear narrative with spare embellishment,
Space structured to give character its feeling
(Faux marble frieze, faux chamber, vaulted ceiling),
And dazzling emissaries, heaven-sent ...

Van Eyck stood right here, Leonardo, too,
Titian and Rubens, Turner, Klee, and Proust
Took tracings for eventual *mots justes*
Washed in this essence, this original blue.

VELÁZQUEZ IN ROME

Galleria Doria Pamphilj

Dispatched to Italy from the Spanish court
To purchase high art of whatever sort
(Statuary, Veronese, Titian),
The man Velázquez accepted a commission
To paint that tough, embittered misanthrope,
The hardly innocent Pamphilj pope,
Driven to place his own grim, taut complexion
Amid the measureless wealth of his collection:
The Laocoön, Apollo Belvedere,
The Stefaneschi Polyptych, the sheer
Heaven of Stanza della Segnatura,
Plus oddities, a camera obscura,
Murals of courtiers with platyrrhini …
Worn out from battles with the Barberini
And flexing the power of the Holy See
To quash the rising Jansenist heresy,
The weary pontiff caught himself reflected
In wariness, arrested and perfected
(Reynolds called it "the finest picture in Rome":
Velázquez carefully took a copy home)
By *manera abreviada*, bold
And vital, mirroring each textured fold
In pinpoint lines, with no soft touch to flatter
The human subject, flawed heart of the matter,
Though subtleties of velvet, linen, silk,
Rich reds and creamy whites (like blood, like milk)
Impart a dignity, if not a grace,
To the shrewd force contracted in that face
Whose owner, seen so clearly, and seen through,
Said only, "*troppo vero*": it is too true.

CÉZANNE IN BALTIMORE

Mont Sainte-Victoire Seen from the Bibémus Quarry
Cone Collection, Baltimore Museum of Art

He painted it, then painted it again
For twenty years or more, week after week
Layering slope, ridge, double limestone peak,
Till rhomboid, trapezoid, block and plane,
Green pines, deep orange cliffs, mauve-tinted sky
Composed an art that's somehow both abstract
And representational: when we react
With five steps back to realign the eye

Space opens in a rush of vertigo
Between the near trees and the quarry wall,
Perspective drops this room, which seemed so small,
Echoing into cavernous effects.
Mont Sainte-Victoire still towers over Aix
Both on and off the canvas· Scene from below.

THE COMPROMISED VENTRILOQUIST

1

Gastromancy, vibration in the gut
    Tuned to the presence of the dead,
Possessed the medium to utter what,
    Digested, triggered hope or dread

In questioners delighted or aghast
    At all they thought they finally knew.
To tell the future or reveal the past
    Was dangerous. The darkest clue

Doomed sacrificial youths and beasts.
    Dim ravings, guttural, abrupt,
Translated to hexameters by priests
    In versions polished and corrupt

Proved riddles no less difficult to crack.
    The truth was rarely clear or kind.
Cautious Lysander wound up stabbed in the back,
    Croesus conquered, Oedipus blind.

THE COMPROMISED VENTRILOQUIST

2

What once was supernatural decree
    Became, in time, a party trick
Crowds at the music halls would pay to see.
    The animated dumb sidekick,

Charlie McCarthy, Sailor Jim, or Coster Joe,
    Though just a cheeky, wiseass puppet,
Would show his straight man up throughout the show,
    Flip every quibble and one up it.

Oracular enshrinement? Oh so past.
    Ventriloquy was entertainment.
Magic was stagecraft, voice the artful cast.
    Nobody wondered what the strain meant.

THE COMPROMISED VENTRILOQUIST

3

Nearing the scribbled end, he took the stage,
    The compromised ventriloquist,
His bare-bones theater the haunted page.
    Obscurity, "uncouthe unkiste,"

Held no protection from the talking dead.
    No charm or curse could exorcise
The choir of sirens singing in his head
    Inspiring another exercise.

His "own distinctive style" at last? Dream on.
    Some stuff he made up, sure. But then
Those ghostly demarcations would stream on
    Flooding his studio again

To wash him up and out and down the drain.
    Too influential, they impressed
And he was pressed. But why complain
    About not being self-possessed?

Conspiring to imprison him for years,
    Through harmony and ornament
The arch conductors of the crystal spheres
    Abused him as their instrument.

Black magic? Maybe. Cheating? Well, that too.
    Who's talking? Uh oh. Hold the phone.
He was the dummy they kept speaking through
    In words that were and weren't his own.

V.

"MY SISTER CUT ME INTO PIECES"

My sister cut me into pieces
    As soon as I was dead.
Worlds upon worlds I'd organized
    She'd organize instead.

My lines grew titles, sprouted rhymes,
    Gained period and "sense,"
And all my artful books were strewn
    By clueless negligence.

And when a man stitched up my leaves,
    With microscopic eye
Aligning all my holes and stains
    Right where they used to lie,

Just as my long-lost reassembled
    Lineaments shone through,
Forgetting all his labor's love
    He rearranged me, too.

"A ROOM OF ZOMBIES SMILED AT ME"

A room of zombies smiled at me
    And offered me a chair,
So I sat down with them. We waited,
    Nowhere and everywhere,

And waited, listening to time,
    Alert though we were dead.
Who were those rapt initiates
    Repeating all we'd said?

"IT'S WHAT'S INSIDE ESTRANGES MOST"

It's what's inside estranges most.
    The landscape of the moon
Would seem just as familiar as
    Our favorite childhood tune

Compared to the immense reserve
    That opens in the mind
Dimensions we can't comprehend.
    Our terms recede behind

Where solitude turns company,
    Where agony seems numb,
When caution triggers recklessness,
    Intelligence stays dumb,

And every burning nerve we have
    Goes marble, petrified,
And we cease half-believing in
    A different world outside.

Out there, back then, in space and time,
    There's something with my name.
People will hear things differently.
    The words sing just the same.

"YOU'LL PAY TO QUOTE A WORD OF MINE"

You'll pay to quote a word of mine.
    The "Dickinson estate"
Returns a profit every line,
    Protectors at the gate

Whose racket is protecting me
    So I can't get to you.
Sister, reader, friend, ephebe,
    The thieves won't let me through!

"I WOULD HAVE LOATHED PUBLICITY"

I would have loathed publicity
    For my most private hopes.
My jottings and imaginings
    On scraps of envelopes

Were never meant to be displayed
    Where anyone could look,
All reproduced on pages of
    A coffee-table book.

But homely, careful, practical
    Economy supplies
An industry of scholarship
    Nothings to fetishize.

What seizure isn't violation?
    What serifed theft not crime?
But Sappho, too, in bits and shards,
    Made her hard way through time

Till every little shred of her,
    Canonical and vast,
Got spread out case by case in The
    Museum of the Past,

Each elemental letter now
    Made flesh, incarnadine,
And she a force field in herself.
    The future is all mine.

"YOU HAVEN'T HEARD THE END OF ME"

You haven't heard the end of me
    By war nor flood nor fire.
I'll take the tops of heads right off,
    I'll twist each nerve to wire

Attuned so waves of sound erode
    The boundaries of sense
And swamp or just obliterate
    All tattered evidence

Of everything you thought you knew
    The simplest thing about,
And consciousness is ocean now,
    And you keep drifting out

Where sea is one big heaving bowl
    And sky its massive twin,
And rising to the wind and waves
    I differ to begin.

So grammar, logic, rhetoric
    Like constellations fall
As I keep figuring—beyond
    Horizon, beyond all.

VI.

IV

HARDY'S WRITING TROUSERS

Where are the hounds who ran the land,
    The Chowders and the Bowsers
      Who bayed at everything,
Or rumbled in a dust-storm of a band
    Swerving right or wrong as
Led by the zig-zag skitters of their prey?
      They had their day.
    They did not last as long as
The piece of raveled, triple-knotted string
That held up Thomas Hardy's writing trousers.

Where are the folk who owned the land,
    The holiday carousers
      Who played at the latest thing,
Whirling together as the village band
    Wound up a final song as
Shalloon and sash and kerchief caught the sway?
      They had their day.
    They did not last as long as
The piece of raveled, triple-knotted string
That held up Thomas Hardy's writing trousers.

Where are the old ones knew the land,
    The forkers, diggers, dowsers
      Who stayed at some hard thing
While fields closed in and pass-through routes were banned,
    With wand and spade and prong as
Busy as if their way were the only way?
      They had their day.
    They did not last as long as
The piece of raveled, triple-knotted string
That held up Thomas Hardy's writing trousers.

THE FORSAKEN SINGER

ACS

When his music defined what the young folk wanted,
When to sing so purely was risky and brave,
And his drop-dead artistry, echo-haunted
By concatenations of wind and wave
Where the foam flower blooms and the sea mew hovers,
Made the high tide fill the most secretive nooks
With studied perfection, true poetry lovers
        Bought his books.

He sang as if there were no tomorrows,
As if past and present were one fluid tense
Full of tacit longings and private sorrows,
As if beauty were meaning and sound were sense.
And all those who heard him were certain they knew
Why he sang as he sang, for a darkling change
Swept over the seascape to render their view
        Rich and strange.

But fashion, as fashioned, falls victim to time.
The polished, percussive extremes of a style
Swirling in arabesque rhythm and rhyme
For a while seemed just right. But just for a while.
What the past most admired the future forecloses.
When the sea winds rise and the sea pines sway
Some things get, like summer's most delicate roses,
        Blown away.

Oh yes he was king of the cats, whose fame
Seemed permanent, scripted by stars. And yet
How many, today, remember his name?
The world doesn't end, but we do forget.
A singer falls silent a hundred years.
Rare bookstores vanish. Small libraries close.
What happens to music when no one hears?
        No one knows.

AUBADE

Recall your gift, my love. Recall
What I so longed for in my youth.
I wanted beauty, thought it truth.
I wanted love, and thought it all.

I thought the ecstasies of song
Whispering immortality
Would ransom me and rescue me
From my old anguish. I was wrong.

But, beautiful, your sunrise steals
In flakes of fire far up the sky.
I tell myself my mourning lie:
Your shining tears, your silver wheels.

LATE AUTUMNAL

Peace. Mists. The sense of something near its end.
Last fruits have fallen, leaves have fallen, too.
Harvest was plumpness, sweetness, swell and bend,
Full-bodied. But that's done. The bees are through.
Winnowing, gleaning, reaping—all are past.
What could be saved has been saved. Now in store
Just coldness, hardness, frost. A light wind dies.
We had enough, and then some. We wanted more
From this, our perfect season which couldn't last.
The stubble darkens. Days are fading fast.
A final swallow, twittering. The skies.

HOBSON'S CHOICE

What needs old Hobson for his broken bones
And girt, his sloughed-off skin? Shifter at last,
Supt on, a ghost of motion, pulled by worms,
No coupled, hobbled load of final terms
Carried too far and stacked like "pilèd stones"
Adds one more breath. Time numbers. Motion past,

He turns up in a phrase, a paradox
Shrewdly maneuvered, weighted, offering
A choice of one, the horse nearest the door
Or none at all. *His* terms, pressed through threescore-
Plus years of riding out a thousand shocks,
Stand witness to his name, though angels sing.

ON TIME

Slow, previous time: with every year your pace
Accelerates, as weeks speed past like hours
Plummeting into darkness and dead space,
Till mind forgets the body's slackened powers.
Each season flips its scenes of sun and rain
      To race aslant across
      Our little field of loss
      And come and go again.
The pleasures the once greedy self consumed
As individual now blur, entombed
In riddled memory; even that kiss
      That seemed the point of bliss,
When two good hearts conjoined for mutual good,
Turns joyless, taken by the darkening flood:
      Our past, dead on the line.
You, signified, present your form. We sign.
      Contracted, monotone,
What makes us happy? Sight, and sight alone,
But less and less. The constellations climb
  The winter sky, and will not quit.
We're tired of stars, the flashing whole of it.
We miss gross earth. And flesh. And chance. And thee o time.

SHAKESPEARE'S HEAD

"That skull had a tongue in it, and could sing once."

1

GOOD FREND FOR IESVS SAKE FORBEARE,
TO DIGG ḚE DVSṪ ENCLOASED HEARE:
BLESE BE Y̦ MAN Y̦ SPARES THES STONES,
AND CVRST BE HE Y̦ MOVES MY BONES.

And cursed be sexton, parish clerk,
Or any man whose dirty work
Disturbs my poor dust where it lies.
I'll see you, though through other eyes.

The dead know how to set things right
Ghosting the corners of the night,
To find and leave you cold in bed,
Your imperfections on your head.

My blessing may do little good
To those refraining as they should,
But if you thrive by doing ill
My curse will mark you, yes it will.

SHAKESPEARE'S HEAD

2

But how to reconcile
The poet of such agony and lust,
Of worldliness, rhetorical bravura,
And infinite variety of style,
    And wit, and *sprezzatura*,
    With this insipid bust

Of bluish Cotswold limestone, set in its niche?
"A self-satisfied pork butcher" (Dover
    Wilson), quill pen in hand,
He looks thick-headed, ordinary, rich.
    Whole worlds at his command?
    The cloud-capp'd show was over.

Fears of the charnel house, of disinterred
Confusion, ossuary mix and match.
    Who's knocked about the mazard,
Chopless? Well, anyone. Without a word
    Poor luck finds out the hazard,
    Some clay a hole to patch.

    Here lies. Commemorate,
Like any other man, the matchless bard.
Like golden lads and girls. The final stage.
"Stay passenger." Regard the name, the date.
    Trust to the living page,
    And pray. The rest is hard.

SHAKESPEARE'S HEAD

3

All your precautions can't anticipate
The odd macabre fads of future days:
The burgeoning celebrity skull craze
That led collectors to decapitate

Beethoven, Haydn, Swift, Sir Thomas Browne,
Geronimo and Goya and de Sade,
Led someone to pry up your stone, then prod
Your resting spot to find you, three feet down,

Shrouded not coffined, and detach their prize.
Ground penetrating radar (GPR)
Discovers you're not where we think you are,
At least your skull is not. To our surprise,

An odd disturbance where your head should be
("A strange brick structure"—what's *that* doing there?)
Suggests an infiltration and repair.
Custodians of Holy Trinity

Won't give permission for an excavation.
With or without your head, they'll let you lie ...
Cue the hideous lines, the shriek owl cry,
The sheeted dead of Gothic machination

Who squeak and gibber, cue men all in fire
Walking the streets like portents, dews of blood,
These late eclipses, wing to th' rooky wood,
Burst cerements. Lights up. Bare ruined choir.

SHAKESPEARE'S HEAD

4

Curse or plea, it matters not.
Greedy finds so Greedy takes,
Scripts the coda, all mistakes.
Mutilation of the plot

Turns romance to tragic farce,
Mocks the poet's dying wish,
Serves his head as on a dish.
Mystery we'll never parse,

Clueless, bootless as the dead.
Property appalled, the self
Reams of paper on a shelf,
Beauty, truth, and all that fled.

Harbinger come far too near,
Invitation in a curse.
Hard, now, to imagine worse.
Like the snows of yesteryear

Constancy is for the birds.
Greedy takes what Greedy finds,
Casts it to the viewless winds.
All's defunctive. Blot these words.

SHAKESPEARE'S HEAD

5

Foul deeds will rise. The heart with strings of steel
Will bow before the altar, flush with guilt.
Confess your sins, though none will be forgiven,
Not heinous theft, nor murderous intent,
Nor profit from imaginary crime.
A magpie's not a man, though black and white,
Blackness of heart, the white of cowardice
Strutting in borrowed feathers, cap-a-pie.
It's better to be vile and vile esteemed
Than not to be, however rank your crimes.

Ladies and gentlemen, *I* stole Shakespeare's head.
At some point in the past, I won't say how
—Strings pulled, palms greased, equipment commandeered—
Jump at the dark-shoaled middle of the night
I slipped past lime trees, found an open door,
By candlelight crowbarred his ledger stone,
Jabbed my right hand right through his threadbare shroud,
Fingered vermicular dust to find his skull
Then gripped it through the eye sockets and took it.
It's sitting on my desk, watching me now.

VII.

DICKENS ON FIRE

Precipitate, determined, absolute
In bending all around him to his will,
    Inflammable and volatile
        And furiously driven,
    Prone to pity and self-pity,
        Oblivious yet acute,
Cruel to his wife, kind to the destitute,
        A man of style
           And skill
        And fueled propensity
    To slog on mile by soggy mile
    Crackling with charged intensity,
        And all the while
Keen eyes fixed on the goals toward which he'd striven,
Fame and its fortunes, charity, Gad's Hill,

Dickens was steadied, somewhat, by routine
Keeping his reckless energy on track,
    A morning shower, quick, ice-cold,
        Then breakfast, then ascending
    To wrestle at his writing desk
        With how to set the scene
For tension, sentiment, an unforeseen
        And manifold
           Attack
    Of twists and turns, grotesque
Incinerations, crimes of old,
    Kind quirks that verge on the burlesque
        Just as they're told
To move the heart, and move it toward an ending,
To keep the pages turning to the back,

DICKENS ON FIRE

(Not to imply his urgent fluency
Spared him the chosen trials of the trade,
    The fundamental restlessness,
        Dead hours, dead days, dead weeks,
    The sharp downspirals of depression
        And pained uncertainty,
The getting up then coming back to see
        What little mess
        We've made
    Or haven't, the obsession
    Guttering till our dark distress
    Snuffs out another hapless session
        Where more is less,
When skies clear, from the valleys rise the peaks,
The dam breaks, and the images cascade),

Then stop for lunch, done writing for the day
At two or three, and after a hearty feed
    Launch vigorous activity,
        A long and fast-paced walk
    Through fields and lanes, or streets and parks,
        Then home to, fiercely, play
At cricket, pocket billiards, or croquet,
        And after tea
        Proceed
    With more communal larks,
    As brisk conviviality
    Strikes brilliant conversational sparks,
        Civility
Brings drink and food and funny games and talk
All wreathed in smoke, according to his need,

DICKENS ON FIRE

Or, if he had the numbers, organize
His family and friends into a troupe
    To take a part and break a leg
        For dramaturgic purpose,
    Staging whatever he'd select
        While he would scrutinize
And drill the children, prompt and tyrannize
          (But never beg)
        The group
    To quickening effect,
    As he, both fuse and powder keg,
    Would blaze away, and thus infect
        Augustus Egg
And Forster and Frank Stone and Uncle Porpoise
Till they would conquer, since they must not stoop,

Or drop by places where he'd find his friends,
The Athenaeum, or the Parthenon,
    The Garrick, where the smoke was thick
        And he could have his say
    Among the clubby tight connections
        Frank *bonhomie* extends,
Denounce what someone mindlessly defends
        Or parry *Sic*
          Et Non,
    Discuss the next elections,
    The latest play, the lunatic
    Love-muddled slapstick indirections
        Of some sidekick
As, effervescent, wired, on high display,
The Sparkler sparkled evenings, on and on,

DICKENS ON FIRE

Or supervise a testimonial
Dinner to benefit some heartfelt cause,
    Old actors or the Ragged Schools,
        Reforming prostitutes,
    Clean water and less filthy air
        (His ceremonial
Issues were native, not colonial),
        To torch the fools'
          Dumb laws
      (Sunday restrictions) where
    Flammable, drain the worst cesspools,
    Build decent housing (Columbia Square),
        Rhetorical tools
    Full bore, "Thanks to you all, thanks to Miss Coutts,"
A last drumroll, the punchline, the applause,

Though for long stretches he would spend his days
On one consuming project (still in his prime,
    Or so he thought, strength could be found,
        Plus he had many bills),
    Like editing a magazine
        For fiction, reviews of plays,
Opinionated letters, brave essays
        To clear the ground,
          The grime,
    The soot, to fix the scene,
    So *Household Words*, then *All the Year Round*
    Would flash together, burnished clean
        And market-bound,
With help from his assistant, W. H. Wills,
Another number, ship-shape, out on time,

DICKENS ON FIRE

Or dragging his Dramatic Company
On tour again (no other thrill would suffice—
    He missed the stage lights, burned to go,
        And tickets always sold
    For amateur theatricals
        Where a happy few could see
A cast of odd, esteemed celebrity
        Braving the snow
            And ice
    To not turn cannibals
  Despite *The Frozen Deep*), just so
    Feeling would fill the meeting halls
        And only grow
To warm his Wardour, dying in the cold,
Rapt with the ardors of self-sacrifice,

And then there were the constant public readings
That drove and drained him through his latter years,
    So lucrative, he would insist
        He must go on despite
    Exhaustion, bravely take the stage
        For ritual proceedings
(Doctors objected, he ignored their pleadings,
        Proudly dismissed
            Their fears),
    The great man of the age
  A spectacle (as he'd persist
    The characters leapt off the page)
        Not to be missed,
The desk, the hat, the gloves, the even light,
The sure crescendo, the held breath, the cheers,

DICKENS ON FIRE

All so addictive, apple of every eye,
Charley was their darling, he was adored,
   They found it riveting, sublime,
      Loved the trial in *Pickwick*,
   Loved to pity the little tykes
     Like Copperfield, whose "I"
Was him, and Tiny Tim, "who did NOT die"
     This Christmastime
      (They roared),
   Shuddered in fear when Sikes
   Would finish Nancy one more time
   (She pleads, he lifts the club, he strikes,
     He flees the crime)
As, murderer and murdered, he felt sick,
His body suffered as their spirits soared,

Then, too, because of or despite it all,
The man was always moving, in nervous flight
   From boredom or mortality,
     To witness, sundry-wise,
   The elemental earthly show,
     Summoned by the call
Of roaring water to watch Niagara fall
     All majesty
      And might
   Shimmer-spanned by rainbow
After rainbow, ceaselessly
Crashing a hundred feet below,
     Where he could see
Tremendous ghosts of spray and mist arise,
Veils of the first things, darkness, depth, God, light,

DICKENS ON FIRE

Or drawn to clamber, one sharp winter night,
Accompanied by guides, his pregnant wife,
   Georgina, "Pickle," a fat stranger,
     Up Mount Vesuvius,
  Intentionally starting late
     To climb in fading light
(He timed it to the moonrise, it was tight)
       Despite all danger
        To life
    And limb, as if dumb fate
  Were some benevolent arranger,
  Though told they really shouldn't wait
     He wouldn't change or
Waver, pressed on ("Good Lord deliver us,"
The sherpas prayed) as wind cut like a knife,

The litters with the women in them veered,
The porters stumbled, cursing, shrieked advice,
   The fat man's litter wobbled, hovered,
    While, creeping, up they went
  (Descent posed the real risk of falling,
    When Pickle disappeared,
Slipping right down a slope that, as he feared,
    Was slickly covered
     In ice,
   Wildly cannonballing
  Out of sight, to be recovered),
  Up where a smoke-filled, sulfurous, appalling
    Plain discovered
Gigantic cinders, with flakes of fire, hell-sent,
Rained down to scorch an anti-paradise,

DICKENS ON FIRE

And where great sheets of flame streamed forth he must,
True to his own wild way, rashly ascend
    To see the molten crater churning,
        Must crawl right to the brim
    And, singeing, linger there (although
        He found having to trust
His weight to the thinness of the trembling crust
        A touch concerning),
           Suspend-
    ed, boiling gulf below,
Then, giddy, roll back down, returning
Blackened, smoking from head to toe,
        His clothes still burning,
But all in every moment, being him,
Dickens on fire, as always, right to the end.

INDEX OF TITLES

A Different Bird	79
"A Room of Zombies Smiled at Me"	356
A Spade a Spade	174
Afghan Kites	210
Air Larry	62
All That's Left	23
Archibald Leach	250
As If	36
At the Grave of Burns	84
Aubade	365
Autopoiesis	314
Catoptric	81
Cézanne in Baltimore	348
Checkered Present	100
Coulrophobia with Line from Auden	338
Damon	256
Dante in Erebus	50
Dante Lost	64
Derecho	309
Dickens on Fire	377
Donal Russell Unbound	53
Dr. Johnson Rolls Down a Hill	226
Easter 2016	335
Echolocation	311
Elegy	133
Elegy for the American Sublime	318
Fidelities	288
For a Season	135
For an Apple Tree	141
For Anthony Hecht	146
For Donald Justice	145
For the Old Women	136
From the Songbook of Henri Provence	34
Frost Heaves	75
Giotto in Padua	346
Gum	164
Hamlet	285
Hardy's Writing Trousers	363
Harrison's Clock	291
Harvest Hobson	343

INDEX OF TITLES

He Wasn't Proust	251
Hearing Voices	282
Henri Provence in Wessex	230
Hikikomori	127
Hobson's Choice	367
Holly Nova Regrets	49
I Hear It Is Charged Against Me	324
"I Would Have Loathed Publicity"	359
Ice Age Art	287
Identity Theft	120
In the Protestant Cemetery in Rome	86
Intimations	143
"It's What's Inside Estranges Most"	357
King Lear	283
Larkin's Nephew	232
Late Autumnal	366
Let Them Say Whatever They Want	322
Like a Ghost I Returned	325
Like Two Men in a Boat	56
Looking for the Lama	87
Lost Punctles	78
Mark Strand	316
Mobile Bay Jubilee	106
My Old Camerado, My Body	327
"My Sister Cut Me into Pieces"	355
Nautical Terms	177
Not Playing Possum	77
Ode	134
Oh	233
On a Line by Wyatt	32
On a Porcelain Bowl	138
On Lethargy	140
On Rereading Some Lines of Poetry	147
On Time	368
Orogenesis	312
Paper View	168
Peregrine Falcon on Skyscraper	96
Plein Air	341
Portrait of the Artist as a Young Kid	253
Returning to the Sea-shore	323

INDEX OF TITLES

River of Song	305
Runaway Blimp	331
Shakespeare's Head	369
Shakespeare's Horse	299
Ship of Trope	163
Sky Burial	281
Some Tuesdays I Go to Lisbon	326
Sometimes I Dream That I Am Not Walt Whitman	321
Song	29
Song of the NRA	334
Sparse Rhymes	245
Stopping	310
Sunday Evening	235
Sunshine and Rain	31
The Albatross	345
The Beautiful Peephole	25
The Catch	117
The Compromised Ventriloquist	349
The Cretonnes of Penelope	26
The Demon Dinanukht	315
The Eccentric Traveler	59
The Ekphrastic Poet	342
The End of Dewitt Finley	66
The End Was Over	317
The Forsaken Singer	364
The Key	240
The Last Book	130
The Lover His Complaint	33
The Place	241
The Relic	82
The Retreat	336
The Site	238
To a House Sparrow	139
To Aeneas Silvius on Monte Amiata	223
To Amaryllis	186
To an Aldabran Tortoise, Dead at 250	183
To Barack Obama	264
To C	201
To False Spring	137
To Gallienus	222

INDEX OF TITLES

To George Washington in Baltimore	188
To His Book	266
To My Friends	196
To Pluto, Upon Its Declassification	207
To Quintus Minimus	221
To Riccardo Duranti	262
To the Republic	187
To the Wind	142
To Trebitsch Lincoln in Hell	268
Touch and Go	165
Trajectory	129
Variation on a Theme by the Weather	27
Velázquez in Rome	347
View of Baltimore from Green Mount Cemetery	89
Virtual Death	125
Wakefield	214
Who They Were	150
Windsock	205
Words on Words	102
"You Haven't Heard the End of Me"	360
"You'll Pay to Quote a Word of Mine"	358
Young Will Shakespeare	103

INDEX OF FIRST LINES

A blue so blue it seems the radiant day	346
A grieving star splashes across the tabloids.	49
A room of zombies smiled at me	356
After some twenty-odd years	117
Ah, Burns, what have they done to ye,	84
All style and substance, elegant and grave,	146
Although	210
Ambitious worldling, ubiquitous diplomat,	223
And what, in the end, can the solitary man	318
Another year is done	133
Archibald Leach was the perfect leading man	250
Arrival of the insects, and the green	34
At home on ledges	96
"By shadowy wall and history-haunted street	86
Cold Amaryllis, don't think I've forgotten,	186
Consider why	143
Dispatched to Italy from the Spanish court	347
Drab avatar of all that's ordinary,	139
Each day we're pummeled by the news.	338
Enter, raving, the demonic Joan of Arc:	103
Even a man of voluminous gravity,	226
Even the most recalcitrant conundrum,	291
Fashioned by firelight, nicked and scooped and planed	287
Faux Oriental blue, your figures faded,	138
From mishap in the King's baker's house	82
Gallienus, buried under centuries	222
Gastromancy, vibration in the gut	349
"Go, for they call you, shepherd, from the hills."	256
GOOD FREND FOR IESVS SAKE FORBEARE,	369
"Guns don't kill people, people do,"	334
Hatred and fear surge on the bitter winds.	335
He opened the largest book, and here they came,	102
He painted it, then painted it again	348
He was a man knew horses, so we moved	299
He was a poet, but the poets who garnered praise	343
Here is the key. The lock is on the door	240
Holding the mirror up, like any art	81
How many years have passed since I last read	147
How stupid Penelope's suitors must have been,	26
"I don't believe you're not on Facebook yet,"	232

INDEX OF FIRST LINES

I hear it is charged against me that I have become an institution,	324
I would have loathed publicity	359
I'd seen him scuttling under a parked car	77
In a diminished corner of New England,	75
In America, it all winds up in court:	53
In London, on his birthday, he went to a play	251
It isn't in the cards: that well-worn phrase	174
It seems, at first, a rudimentary art	168
It snowed. Now, self-defeated by conquest,	336
It was a life of sorts, alone on the road.	66
It was no dream, I lay broad waking	32
It's quiet here. A stoic rectitude	285
It's what's inside estranges most.	357
Just as the bottlenose or pipistrelle	311
Just walking along the street this warm spring day,	31
Let Dominica be the essence of green,	201
Let me begin, as if there never were	36
Let them say whatever they want about me on the Internet,	322
Let's not pretend we don't know how he felt,	125
Lift all the summer's green epiphanies,	142
Like a ghost I returned to my old house in Camden	325
Like the first cold trickles to slip	29
Long years have passed, but I still grieve,	150
May all the vulnerable young	221
My friend Riccardo, you are a lucky fellow	262
My good friends, when you're under the illusion	196
My old camerado, my body, how long has it been?	327
My sister cut me into pieces	355
Nature alone is perfect. In the woods	59
Not all that long ago,	177
Now, when the thatch-roofed cottages	230
Nyssa or Liquidambar, Eucalyptus,	164
O build your ship of trope, for you will need it.	163
O elevated visionary thoughts,	134
O TRAVELER TURN BACK WHEN YOU ARRIVE	50
Of course some wise guy *would* nickname him "King,"	283
Often, to amuse themselves, the sailors seize	345
On a calm night, in summer or early fall,	106
On daily walks I'd seen	331
On the radio today they estimated	27

INDEX OF FIRST LINES

Out for a walk	79
Peace. Mists. The sense of something near its end.	366
Precipitate, determined, absolute	377
Projects of a dubious nature were undertaken	100
Recall your gift, my love. Recall	365
Returning to the sea-shore after more than a century	323
Skirting disaster, walking a very fine line	165
Slow, previous time: with every year your pace	368
So why on earth set sail	56
Some truths it might be shrewder *not* to tell.	314
Some Tuesdays I go to Lisbon to see my friend Álvaro de Campos.	326
Somehow the pieces clicked at the right time,	135
Something catches the corner of the eye,	87
Sometimes I dream that I am not Walt Whitman,	321
Start with the moral: the fabric of our lives,	214
Such things were treasured objects, long ago,	130
Sunk in his chair, he seems half man, half book,	315
The beautiful peephole lets us see the way	25
The ekphrastic poet seeks a fine vignette	342
The end was over, over long ago.	317
The landlord's murdered you. Your trunk's been bored,	141
The night is clear, without the slightest wind,	235
The nineteenth century	89
The perils of our hyperdigital age	120
The races of the swift,	183
The word is out you're out, the ninth of nine	207
The years have failed us, as you knew they would.	145
There they were in the basement, the whole troop	253
They've sent him in again, and now he's stuck	64
This conical textile tube to show	205
Though the phenomenon is Japanese,	127
Too tired to write, to read, to anything!	140
We didn't know the word, until it raced	309
We'd like to think the marks that mark our pauses,	78
Welcome to the site. There is no need	238
What have we done, who once were hailed	187
What *is* this landscape, rising like a dream	341
What needs old Hobson for his broken bones	367
Whatever piece of code,	288
When his music defined what the young folk wanted,	364

INDEX OF FIRST LINES

When I came to the end of the dream, there was Mark Strand.	316
When I was a young man	245
When Ishmael, perched high	188
When love herself came to me	233
When moonstruck spirits said	312
When the idea came	62
Where are the hounds who ran the land,	363
Where are they gone, the old women bent double,	136
Where in Hell would Dante Alighieri	268
Wherever the soul goes,	281
Who *said* that?	305
Who were we, back before the whole world changed?	129
Whose voice is this, just audible through static?	282
Whose woods these are we all know well	310
Will someone tell me, please,	23
You haven't heard the end of me	360
You left me years ago, and ever since,	33
You seem to want, my book, to be out on our own,	266
You'll never find the place, but you must try.	241
You'll pay to quote a word of mine.	358
You've tricked the flowers out	137
You've written me, once again, to ask for money.	264

ACKNOWLEDGMENTS

Grateful acknowledgment is made to the following publications in which many of the poems in this volume originally appeared:

Alabama Literary Review, The American Scholar, The Antioch Review, Arion, The Best American Poetry 1998, Birmingham Poetry Review, Boston Review, Center, The Common, The Hopkins Review, The Hudson Review, The Kenyon Review, Literary Matters, Measure, The New Criterion, The New York Review of Books, nuovo argomenti, The Paris Review, Parnassus, Le Parole e le Cose, Passager, Poetry Northwest, Poets.org, Raritan, River Styx, The Sewanee Review, Sewanee Theological Review, Smartish Pace, Southern Humanities Review, Southwest Review, Unsplendid.com, The Yale Review.

The author would also like to thank all those who gave encouragement, made suggestions, or otherwise helped in the preparation of this book, especially Robert Schreur, Eric McHenry, Stephen Kampa, Philip Hoy, and Morri Creech.

A NOTE ABOUT THE AUTHOR

Joseph Harrison was born in Richmond, Virginia, grew up in Virginia and Alabama, and took degrees at Yale and Johns Hopkins. He is the author of six previous books of poetry, including the four Waywiser collections—*Someone Else's Name* (2003), *Identity Theft* (2008), *Shakespeare's Horse* (2015), and *Sometimes I Dream That I Am Not Walt Whitman* (2020)—brought together in this volume. *Someone Else's Name* was named one of five poetry books of the year by *The Washington Post* and was a finalist for the Poets' Prize; *Shakespeare's Horse* was also a finalist for the Poets' Prize. He has received a Guggenheim fellowship in poetry and an Academy Award in Literature from the American Academy of Arts and Letters, among other honors.

Mr. Harrison was director of the Anthony Hecht Poetry Prize from its inception in 2006 until 2022. He edited *The Hecht Prize Anthology* (2010) and, with Damiano Abeni, *Un mondo che non può essere migliore: Poesie scelte 1956-2007* (2008), a selection from the poetry of John Ashbery that won a Special Prize from the Premio Napoli. He lives in Baltimore, where he teaches privately and works as an editor.

OTHER BOOKS FROM WAYWISER

POETRY

Austin Allen, *Pleasures of the Game*
Al Alvarez, *New & Selected Poems*
Chris Andrews, *Lime Green Chair*
Danielle Blau, *peep*
Audrey Bohanan, *Any Keep or Contour*
George Bradley, *A Few of Her Secrets*
Geoffrey Brock, *Voices Bright Flags*
Christopher Cessac, *The Youngest Ocean*
Robert Conquest, *Blokelore & Blokesongs*
Robert Conquest, *Collected Poems*
Robert Conquest, *Penultimata*
Morri Creech, *Blue Rooms*
Morri Creech, *Field Knowledge*
Morri Creech, *The Sleep of Reason*
James D'Agostino, *The Goldfinch Caution Tapes*
Peter Dale, *One Another*
James Davis, *Club Q*
Erica Dawson, *Big-Eyed Afraid*
B. H. Fairchild, *The Art of the Lathe*
David Ferry, *On This Side of the River: Selected Poems*
Daniel Groves & Greg Williamson, eds., *Jiggery-Pokery Semicentennial*
Jeffrey Harrison, *The Names of Things: New & Selected Poems*
Joseph Harrison, *Identity Theft*
Joseph Harrison, *Shakespeare's Horse*
Joseph Harrison, *Someone Else's Name*
Joseph Harrison, *Sometimes I Dream That I Am Not Walt Whitman*
Joseph Harrison, ed., *The Hecht Prize Anthology, 2005-2009*
Anthony Hecht, *Collected Later Poems*
Anthony Hecht, *The Darkness and the Light*
Jaimee Hills, *How to Avoid Speaking*
Katherine Hollander, *My German Dictionary*
Hilary S. Jacqmin, *Missing Persons*
Carrie Jerrell, *After the Revival*
Stephen Kampa, *Articulate as Rain*
Stephen Kampa, *Bachelor Pad*
Rose Kelleher, *Bundle o' Tinder*
Mark Kraushaar, *The Uncertainty Principle*
Matthew Ladd, *The Book of Emblems*
J. D. McClatchy, *Plundered Hearts: New and Selected Poems*
Dora Malech, *Shore Ordered Ocean*
Jérôme Luc Martin, *The Gardening Fires: Sonnets and Fragments*
Eric McHenry, *Odd Evening*
Eric McHenry, *Potscrubber Lullabies*
Eric McHenry and Nicholas Garland, *Mommy Daddy Evan Sage*
Timothy Murphy, *Very Far North*
Ian Parks, *Shell Island*
V. Penelope Pelizzon, *Whose Flesh is Flame, Whose Bone is Time*
Hannah Louise Poston, *Julia Hungry*
Chris Preddle, *Cattle Console Him*
Shelley Puhak, *Guinevere in Baltimore*
Christopher Ricks, ed., *Joining Music with Reason:
34 Poets, British and American, Oxford 2004-2009*
Daniel Rifenburgh, *Advent*
Mary Jo Salter, *It's Hard to Say: Selected Poems*

OTHER BOOKS FROM WAYWISER

Alan Shapiro, *By and By*
W. D. Snodgrass, *Not for Specialists: New & Selected Poems*
Mark Strand, *Almost Invisible*
Mark Strand, *Blizzard of One*
Bradford Gray Telford, *Perfect Hurt*
Matthew Thorburn, *This Time Tomorrow*
Cody Walker, *Shuffle and Breakdown*
Cody Walker, *The Self-Styled No-Child*
Cody Walker, *The Trumpiad*
Henry Walters, *The Nature Thief*
Deborah Warren, *The Size of Happiness*
Clive Watkins, *Already the Flames*
Clive Watkins, *Jigsaw*
Richard Wilbur, *Anterooms*
Richard Wilbur, *Mayflies*
Richard Wilbur, *Collected Poems 1943-2004*
Norman Williams, *One Unblinking Eye*
Greg Williamson, *A Most Marvelous Piece of Luck*
Greg Williamson, *The Hole Story of Kirby the Sneak and Arlo the True*
Stephen Yenser, *Stone Fruit*

FICTION

Gregory Heath, *The Entire Animal*
Mary Elizabeth Pope, *Divining Venus*
K. M. Ross, *The Blinding Walk*
Gabriel Roth, *The Unknowns**
Matthew Yorke, *Chancing It*

ILLUSTRATED

Nicholas Garland, *I wish ...*
Eric McHenry and Nicholas Garland, *Mommy Daddy Evan Sage*
Greg Williamson, *The Hole Story of Kirby the Sneak and Arlo the True*

NON-FICTION

Neil Berry, *Articles of Faith: The Story of British Intellectual Journalism*
Irving Feldman, *Usable Truths: Aphorisms & Observations*
Mark Ford, *A Driftwood Altar: Essays and Reviews*
Philip Hoy, *M. Degas Steps Out: An Essay*
Philip Hoy, ed., *A Bountiful Harvest: The Correspondence of Anthony Hecht and William L. MacDonald*
John Rosenthal, *Searching for Amylu Danzer*
Richard Wollheim, *Germs: A Memoir of Childhood*

*Co-published with Picador